D1500308

BALLAD BOOK

BALLAD BOOK

EDITED BY

KATHARINE LEE BATES

"The plaintive numbers flow
For old, unhappy, far-off things,
And battles long ago."

WILLIAM WORDSWORTH.

Granger Index Reprint Series

BOOKS FOR LIBRARIES PRESS
FREEPORT, NEW YORK

First Published 1890
Reprinted 1969

821.008
B32 b

STANDARD BOOK NUMBER:
8369-6096-3

LIBRARY OF CONGRESS CATALOG CARD NUMBER:
78-103081

MANUFACTURED
BY
HALLMARK LITHOGRAPHERS, INC.
IN THE U.S.A.

PREFACE.

Probably no teacher of English literature in our schools or colleges would gainsay the statement that one chief aim of such instruction is to awaken in the student a genuine love and enthusiasm for the higher forms of prose, and more especially for poetry. For love is the surest guarantee of extended and independent study, and we teachers are the first to admit that the class-room is but the vestibule to education. So in beginning the critical study of English poetry it seems reasonable to use as a starting-point the early ballads, belonging as they do to the youth of our literature, to the youth of our English race, and hence appealing with especial fascination to the youth of the human heart. Every man of letters who still retains the boy-element in his nature — and most men, Sir Philip Sidney tells us, are "children in the best things, till they be cradled in their graves" — has a tenderness for these rough, frank, spirited old poems, while the actual boy in years, or the actual girl, rarely fails to respond to their charm.

iii

What Shakespeare knew, and Scott loved, and Mac-Donald echoes, can hardly be beneath the admiration of high school and university students. Rugged language, broken metres, absurd plots, dubious morals, are powerless to destroy the vital beauty that underlies all these. There is a philosophical propriety, too, in beginning poetic study with ballad lore, for the ballad is the germ of all poem varieties. From it are successively developed the epic, lyric, and drama.

This volume attempts to present such a selection from the old ballads as shall represent them fairly in their three main classes, — those derived from superstition, whether fairy-lore, witch-lore, ghost-lore, or demon-lore; those derived from tradition, Scotch and English; and those derived from romance and from domestic life in general. The Scottish ballads, because of their far superior poetic value, are found here in greater number than the English. The notes state in each case what version has been followed.

The introduction deals with various questions bearing upon the ballads as a whole — the trend of poem development, the probable antiquity and the literary history of our Scotch and English ballads, and the relation of modern ballads to ancient. Lists are given of our best ballad collections, of representative modern ballads, and of those ballads in this volume for which versions are

found in other literatures. Methods of study and recitation in ballad work are suggested. The notes aim to
give such facts of historical or bibliographical impor-
tance as may attach to each ballad, with any indispens-
able explanation of outworn or dialectic phrases, although
here much is left to the mother-wit of the student.

It is hoped that this selection may meet a definite
need in connection with classes not so fortunate as to
have access to a ballad library, and that even where
such access is procurable, it may prove a friendly
companion in the private study and the recitation-room.

KATHARINE LEE BATES.

Wellesley College,
    May, 1890.

CONTENTS.

	PAGE
INTRODUCTION	ix

BALLADS OF SUPERSTITION.

THE WEE WEE MAN	3
TAMLANE	4
TRUE THOMAS	12
THE ELFIN KNIGHT	15
LADY ISOBEL AND THE ELF-KNIGHT	18
TOM THUMBE	21
KEMPION	33
ALISON GROSS	37
THE WIFE OF USHER'S WELL	39
A LYKE-WAKE DIRGE	41
PROUD LADY MARGARET	43
THE TWA SISTERS O' BINNORIE	48
THE DEMON LOVER	53
RIDDLES WISELY EXPOUNDED	56

BALLADS OF TRADITION.

SIR PATRICK SPENS	61
THE BATTLE OF OTTERBURNE	65
THE HUNTING OF THE CHEVIOT	71
EDOM O' GORDON	83
KINMONT WILLIE	89
KING JOHN AND THE ABBOT OF CANTERBURY	97
ROBIN HOOD RESCUING THE WIDOW'S THREE SONS	101
ROBIN HOOD AND ALLIN A DALE	106
ROBIN HOOD'S DEATH AND BURIAL	111

ROMANTIC AND DOMESTIC BALLADS.

PAGE

ANNIE OF LOCHROYAN 117
LORD THOMAS AND FAIR ANNET 123
THE BANKS O' YARROW 129
THE DOUGLAS TRAGEDY 133
FINE FLOWERS I' THE VALLEY 136
THE GAY GOSS-HAWK 140
YOUNG REDIN 145
WILLIE AND MAY MARGARET 150
YOUNG BEICHAN 155
GILDEROY 162
BONNY BARBARA ALLAN 166
THE GARDENER 168
ETIN THE FORESTER 169
LAMKIN 177
HUGH OF LINCOLN 182
FAIR ANNIE 185
THE LAIRD O' DRUM 189
LIZIE LINDSAY 192
KATHARINE JANFARIE 196
GLENLOGIE 199
GET UP AND BAR THE DOOR 201
THE LAWLANDS O' HOLLAND 203
THE TWA CORBIES 204
HELEN OF KIRCONNELL 205
WALY WALY 207
LORD RONALD 208
EDWARD, EDWARD 209

INTRODUCTION.

THE development of poetry, the articulate life of man, is hidden of necessity in that morning mist which overhangs the early centuries of human history. Yet the indications are that this art of arts had its origin, as far back as the days of savagery, in the ideal element of life rather than the utilitarian. There came a time, undoubtedly, when the mnemonic value of verse was recognized in the transmission of laws and records and the hard-won wealth of experience. Our own Anglo-Saxon ancestors, whose rhyme, it will be remembered, was initial rhyme, or alliteration, have bequeathed to our modern speech many such devices for "the knitting up of the memory," largely legal or popular phrases, as *bed and board, to have and to hold, to give and to grant, time and tide, wind and wave, gold and gear;* or proverbs, as for example: *When bale is highest, boon is nighest,* better known to the present age under the still alliterative form: *The darkest hour's before the dawn.* But if we may trust the signs of poetic evolution in barbarous tribes to-day, if we may draw inferences from the sacred character attached to the Muses in the myths of all races, with the old Norsemen, for instance, Sagâ being the daughter of Odin, we may rest a reasonable confidence upon the theory that poetry, the world over, finds its first utterance at the bidding of the religious instinct and in connection with religious rites.

Yet the wild-eyed warriors, keeping time by a rude triumphal chant to the dance about the watch-fire, are mentally as children, with keen senses and eager imagination, but feeble reason, with fresh and vigorous emotions, but without elaborate language for these emotions. This half-inarticulate pæan, as with the process of time it resolves itself into an ordered poem, does not take the lyric form of direct praise to the god who has won his votaries the victory, nor does it give direct expression to their rejoicing. It honors the hero-god by singing his great life-story, or it perpetuates the joy of the "war-wolves" by telling over the deeds of the battle-field. Hence the popular epic antedates the pure lyric, and we have the Nibelungen Lied — in its primitive forms, at least — before the songs of the Minnesingers, the Iliad before the odes of Sappho.

Yet surely in the Nibelungen Lied and possibly in the Iliad we deal with but a skilfully welded collection of ballads, the elder epics having come into being by a process of natural growth, not of arbitrary construction. We have but to compare the Cid with the Aeneid, Beowulf with the Paradise Lost, to feel the difference between the ballad-born poem of a people, and the literary masterpiece of a man.

In our own literature, from the day of Chaucer down, we have had but one marked ballad-group promising a popular epic, and this has proven a case of arrested development. The Robin Hood ballads have waited so long for the moulding hand of a master, that the English spirit has well-nigh grown out of sympathy with their greenwood life and their bluff, rollicking hero. For English literature has not been left free to work out its own salvation. French story, Italian song, Hellenic grace, Hebraic passion, German thought, have pressed too close upon it. Foreign influence and ancient example did with bewildering rapidity for the singers of the court and the university what the slow culture of time was scarcely beginning to do for the singers of the populace. Our English poetry comes too late in the world's history to stand as an example of the normal development of the poetic germ.

None the less, our early ballads, the most of them bearing, as they do, in Teutonic dialect and democratic spirit, traces of a popular origin, without claim of date or individual authorship, preserved for centuries by oral transmission, are legitimate examples, in this precocious, press-driven literature of ours, of the primitive poems that are born, not made. Even so comparatively small a group as that comprehended within this volume shows how truly the ballad is the parent stock of all other poem forms. In the ballad of plain narrative, as *The Hunting of the Cheviot*, the epic is hinted. We go a step further in *A Lytell Geste of Robyn Hode*, — too long for insertion in this collection, but peculiarly interesting from the antiquarian point of view, having been printed as early as 1489, — and find at least a rough foundation for a genuine hero-song, the *Lytell Geste* being made up of a number of ballads rudely woven into one. A poem like this, though hardly "an epic in miniature," — a phrase which has been proposed as the definition of a ballad, — is truly an epic in germ, lacking the finish of a miniature, but holding the promise of a seed. Where the narrative is highly colored by emotion, as in *Helen of Kirconnell* or *Waly Waly*, the ballad merges into the lyric. It is difficult here to draw the line of distinction. *A Lyke-Wake Dirge* is almost purely lyric in quality, while *The Lawlands o' Holland, Gilderoy, The Twa Corbies, Bonny Barbara Allan*, have each a pronounced lyric element. From the ballad of dialogue we look forward to the drama, not only from the ballad of pure dialogue, as *Lord Ronald*, or *Edward, Edward*, or that sweet old English folk-song, too long for insertion here, *The Not-Browne Mayd*, but more remotely from the ballad of mingled dialogue and narrative, as *The Gardener* or *Fine Flowers i' the Valley*.

Yet while epic, lyric, and drama are all inherent in the ballad, we must not forget that in England these poetic varieties were introduced from without, not left to the slow development from within. But nevertheless, while Dan Chaucer, his genius fed by Norman and Italian streams, was making the fourteenth century re-echo with that laughter which "comes never to an end" of the Canterbury story-tellers; while Long Will, even his Teutonic spirit swayed by French example, was wrenching from his broken heart the gloomy "Vision of Piers the Plowman," — gloom with a star at its centre; while those "courtly makers," Wyatt and Surrey, were smoothing English song, which in the hands of Skelton had become so

> " Tatter'd and jagged,
> Rudely raine-beaten,
> Rusty and moth-eaten,"

into the exquisite lyrical measures of Italy ; while the dull, grotesque old mysteries and miracle-plays, also of Continental impulse, were still, in all innocence of the coming rupture between Church and Stage, striving to do God service by impressing the Scripture stories upon their rustic audiences, — the ballads were being sung and told from Scottish loch to English lowland, in hamlet and in hall. Heartily enjoyed in the baronial castle, scandalously well known in the monastery, they were dearest to the peasants.

> " Lewd peple loven tales olde ;
> Swiche thinges can they wel report and holde."

The written form in which we possess these ballads to-day is comparatively modern. Few can be dated further back than the reign of Elizabeth; the language of some is that of the last century. But the number and variety of versions — the ballad of *Lord Ronald*, for instance, being given in fifteen forms by Professor Child in his monumental edition of " The English and Scottish Popular Ballads ; " " Lord Ronald, my son," appearing variously as " Lord Randal, my son," " Lord Donald, my son," " King Henrie, my son," " Lairde Rowlande, my son," " Billy, my son," " Tiranti, my son," " my own pretty boy," " my bonnie wee croodlin dow," " my little wee croudlin doo," "Willie doo, Willie doo," "my wee wee croodlin doo doo," — are sure evidence of oral transmission, and oral transmission is in itself evidence of antiquity. Other indications of oral transmission are the liberties taken with accent, as harpèr, battèl, ladiè, the inaccuracies in rhyme and roughnesses in metre, which could be partially disguised by the voice, and the memory-easing refrains and stock stanzas. But the venerable age of our ballads is best realized through the remoteness of the events they record. Occasionally we can fix a date to the deed, as for instance it is tolerably certain that the heroic and ill-fated voyage of Sir Patrick Spens took place in 1281. Frequently we can determine the period in which a ballad originated, by its feudal setting and mediæval color. The antiquity of our oldest ballads, however, is established by the fact that similar folk-songs on the same topics are to be found in the literatures not only of European countries, especially the Scandinavian, but often of Asiatic countries as well. Before such groups of strangely kindred ballads, so alike in their unlikeness, the mind marvels, sending a lonely thought far back to the Oriental dawn-life of our race, but hazards no assertion. The ballads in this collection, for which equivalents have thus far been discovered in the folk-lore of Continental Europe, or of Asia, or of both, are the following:

Alison Gross.
A Lyke-Wake Dirge.
Edward, Edward.
Etin the Forester.   (Hynd Etin.)

Fair Annie.

Fine Flowers i' the Valley. (The Cruel Brother.)

Hugh of Lincoln. (Sir Hugh, or the Jew's Daughter.)

Katharine Janfarie. (Catharine Johnstone.)

Kempion. (Kemp Owain.)

Lady Isobel and the Elf-Knight. (May Colvin.) (Fause Sir John.) (The Water o' Wearie's Well.)

Lord Ronald. (Lord Randal.) (Willie Doo.)

Lord Thomas and Fair Annet. (Lord Thomas and Fair Ellinor.) (Sweet Willie and Fair Annie.) (The Nut-Brown Bride.)

Riddles Wisely Expounded.

The Douglas Tragedy. (Earl Brand.)

The Elfin Knight. (The Fairy Knight.) (Lord John.) (The Deil's Courtship.)

The Twa Sisters o' Binnorie. (The Cruel Sister.) (The Miller and the King's Daughter.) (The Bonnie Mill-dams of Binnorie.)

Young Beichan. (Young Bekie.) (Lord Bateman.) (Lord Beichan and Susie Pye.)

The mere enumeration of these brave old ballads calls up the picture of the wandering bards who for generations passed them down from lip to lip. Before the imagination passes

> " Each Caledonian minstrel true,
>   Dressed in his plaid and bonnet blue,
>   With harp across his shoulders slung,
>   And music murmuring round his tongue."

Fearless children of nature these strolling poets were, even as the songs they sang.

> " Little recked they, our bards of old,
>   Of autumn's showers, or winter's cold.
>   Sound slept they on the 'nighted hill,
>   Lulled by the winds, or bubbling rill,
>   Curtained within the winter cloud,
>   The heath their couch, the sky their shroud;
>   Yet theirs the strains that touch the heart, —
>   Bold, rapid, wild, and void of art."

The value and hence the dignity of the minstrel's profession declined with the progress of the printing-press in popular favor, and the character of the gleemen suffered in consequence. This was more marked in England than in Scotland. Indeed, the question has been raised as to whether there ever existed a class of Englishmen who were both ballad-singers and ballad-makers. This was one of the points at issue between those eminent antiquarians, Bishop Percy and Mr. Ritson, in the last century. Dr. Percy had defined the English minstrels as an "order of men in the middle ages, who subsisted by the arts of poetry and music, and sung to the harp the verses which they themselves composed." The inflammable Joseph Ritson, whose love of an honest ballad goes far to excuse him for his lack of loving demeanor toward the unfaithful editor of the *Reliques,* pounced down so fiercely upon this definition, contending that, however applicable to Icelandic skalds or Norman trouvères or Provençal troubadours, it was altogether too flattering for the vagabond fiddlers of England, roughly trolling over to tavern audiences the ballads borrowed from their betters, that the dismayed bishop altered his last clause to read, "verses composed by themselves or others."

Sir Walter Scott sums up this famous quarrel with his characteristic good-humor. "The debate," he says, " resembles the apologue of the gold and silver shield. Dr. Percy looked on the minstrel in the palmy and exalted state to which, no doubt, many were elevated by their talents, like those who possess excellence in the fine arts in the present day; and Ritson considered the reverse of the medal, when the poor and wandering gleeman was glad to purchase his bread by singing his ballads at the ale-house, wearing a fantastic habit, and latterly sinking into a mere crowder upon an untuned fiddle, accompanying his rude strains with a ruder ditty, the helpless associate of drunken revellers, and marvellously afraid of the constable and parish beadle."

There is proof enough that, by the reign of Elizabeth, the printer was elbowing the minstrel out into the gutter. In Scotland the strolling bard was still not without honor, but in the sister country we find him denounced by ordinance together with " rogues, vagabonds, and sturdy beggars." The London stalls were fed by Grub-street authors with penny ballads — trash for the greater part — printed in black-letter on broadsides. Many of these precious productions were collected into small miscellanies, known as *Garlands*, in the reign of James I.; but few of the genuine old folk-songs found a refuge in print. Yet they still lived on in corners of England and Scotland, where "the spinsters and the knitters in the sun" crooned over half-remembered lays to peasant children playing at their feet.

In 1723 a collection of English ballads, made up

largely, though not entirely, of stall-copies, was issued by an anonymous editor, not a little ashamed of himself because of his interest in so unworthy a subject; for although Dryden and Addison had played the man and given kindly entertainment — the one in his *Miscellany Poems,* the other in *The Spectator* — to a few ballad-gypsies, yet poetry in general, that most "flat, stale, and unprofitable" poetry of the early and middle eighteenth century, disdained all fellowship with the unkempt, wandering tribe.

In the latter half of this century, however, occurred the great event in the history of ballad literature. The last son of the ancient house of Percy — a name rich with memories of "Otterburn" and "Chevy Chase" — being on a visit to his "worthy friend, Humphrey Pitt, Esq., then living at Shiffnal in Shropshire," had the glorious good luck to hit upon an old folio manuscript of ballads and romances. "I saw it," writes Percy, "lying dirty on the floor under a Bureau in ye Parlour; being used by the Maids to light the fire."

"A scrubby, shabby paper book" it may have been, with some leaves torn half away and others lacking altogether, but it was a genuine ballad manuscript, in handwriting of about the year 1650, and Percy, realizing that the worthy Mr. Pitt was feeding his parlor fire with very expensive fuel, begged the tattered volume of his host and bore it proudly home, where with presumptuous pen he revised and embellished and otherwise, all innocently, maltreated the noble old ballads until he deemed, although with grave misgivings, that they would not too violently shock the polite taste of the eighteenth century. The eighteenth century, wearied to death of its own politeness, worn out by the heartless elegance of Pope and the insipid sentimentality of Prior, gave these fresh, simple melodies an unexpected wel come, even in the face of the reigning king of letters, Dr Johnson, who forbade them to come to court. But good poems are not slain by bad critics, and the old ballads, despite the burly doctor's displeasure, took henceforth a recognized place in English literature. Herd's delightful collection of Scottish songs and ballads, wherein are gathered so many of those magical refrains, the rough ore of Burns' fine gold — " Green grow the rashes O," " Should auld acquaintance be forgot," "For the sake o' somebody," — soon followed, and Ritson, while ever slashing away at poor Percy, often for his minstrel theories, more often for his ballad emendations, and most often for his holding back the original folio manuscript from publication, appeared himself as a collector and antiquarian of admirable quality. Mean- while Walter Scott, still in his schoolboy days, had chanced upon a copy of the *Reliques*, and had fallen in love with ballads at first sight. All the morning long he lay reading the book beneath a huge platanus-tree in his aunt's garden. "The summer day sped onward so fast," he says, " that notwithstanding the sharp appetite of thirteen, I forgot the hour of dinner, was sought for with anxiety, and was found still entranced in my intel- lectual banquet. To read and to remember was in this instance the same thing, and henceforth I overwhelmed my school-fellows and all who would hearken to me, with tragical recitations from the ballads of Bishop Percy. The first time, too, I could scrape a few shillings together, which were not common occurrences with me, I bought unto myself a copy of these beloved volumes, nor do I believe I ever read a book half so frequently, or with half the enthusiasm."

The later fruits of that schoolboy passion were garnered in Scott's original ballads, metrical romances, and no less romantic novels, all so picturesque with feudal lights and shadows, so pure with chivalric sentiment; but an earlier result was *The Minstrelsy of the Scottish Border,* a collection of folk-songs gleaned in vacation excursions from pipers and shepherds and old peasant women of the border districts, and containing, with other ballads, full forty-three previously unknown to print, among them some of our very best. Other poet collectors — Motherwell and Aytoun — followed where Scott had led, Scott having been himself preceded by Allan Ramsay, who so early as 1724 had included several old ballads, freely retouched, in his *Evergreen* and *Tea-Table Miscellany.* Nor were there lacking others, poets in ear and heart if not in pen, who went up and down the country-side, seeking to gather into books the old heroic lays that were already on the point of perishing from the memories of the people. Meanwhile Ritson's shrill cry for the publication of the original Percy manuscript was taken up in varying keys again and again, until in our own generation the echoes on our own side of the water grew so persistent that with no small difficulty the much-desired end was actually attained. The owners of the folio having been brought to yield their slow consent, our richest treasure of Old English song, for so perilously long a period exposed to all the hazards that beset a single manuscript, is safe in print at last and open to the inspection of us all. Professor Child, our first American authority on ballad-lore, and Mr. Furnivall, that indefatigable scholar whose very name carries a wave of Old English enthusiasm with it, would each yield the other the honor of this achievement for which no ballad-lover can speak too many thanks.

A list of our principal ballad collections may be found of practical convenience, as well as of literary interest. Passing by the *Miscellanies*, Percy, as becomes one of his gallant lineage, leads the van.

Percy's Reliques of Ancient English Poetry. 1765.
Herd's Ancient and Modern Scottish Songs, Heroic Ballads, etc. 1769.
Ritson's Ancient Popular Poetry. 1791.
Ritson's Ancient Songs and Ballads. 1792.
Ritson's Robin Hood. 1795.
Scott's Minstrelsy of the Scottish Border. 1802–1803.
Jamieson's Popular Ballads and Songs. 1806.
Finlay's Scottish Historical and Romantic Ballads. 1808.
Sharpe's Ballad Book. 1824.
Maidment's North Countrie Garland. 1824.
Kinloch's Ancient Scottish Ballads. 1827.
Motherwell's Minstrelsy, Ancient and Modern. 1827.
Buchan's Ancient Ballads and Songs of the North of Scotland. 1828.
Chambers' Scottish Ballads. 1829.

Whitelaw's Book of Scottish Ballads. 1845.
Child's English and Scottish Ballads. 1857–1858.
Aytoun's Ballads of Scotland. 1858.
Maidment's Scotish Ballads and Songs. 1868.
Bishop Percy's Folio Manuscript. 1868.
Child's English and Scottish Popular Ballads (issued in
    parts). 1882–.

It is a rare experience nowadays to meet with Dr.
Johnson, — with a critic who, knowing the early folk-
songs of our literature, fails to love them. Far more
commonly we encounter the opinion that the only ballad is an old ballad; that the nineteenth century pre-
tends in vain to the strolling minstrel's art: that the
frank, unconscious ballad-note has passed from our
poetry forever. At this point there is no resort but a
definition. If we call a ballad a narrative poem, true to
the simplest phases of nature, art, and life, we have
something on which to build an argument for the possi-
bility of modern ballads. But if we insist on that
impalpable yet positive element, strange and sweet and
far away, warm as heart-blood, deeper than design, —
that element inherent in our old ballads from the very
peculiarity of their origin and growth; that quintessence
of vitality concentrated from the many voices of long
ago by which they have been sung into their present
forms; that wistful, woeful beauty flushed across them
from the human faith and sympathy of all these listen-
ing generations, we obviously insist on what no individual author can impart. A short list of selected modern
poems that may claim, if any such may claim, to be

ranked as ballads, is subjoined, and the discussion passed
over to whomsoever cares to take it up.

Scott's The Gray Brother.
Motherwell's The Ettin o' Sillarwood.
Aytoun's The Execution of Montrose.
Hogg's The Witch of Fife.
MacDonald's The Earl o' Quarter-deck.
Coleridge's The Rime of the Ancient Mariner.
Wordsworth's Lucy Gray.
Keats' La Belle Dame sans Merci.
Macaulay's The Battle of Naseby.
Rossetti's The King's Tragedy.
Buchanan's The Ballad of Judas Iscariot.
Jean Ingelow's Winstanley.
Swinburne's The Bride's Tragedy.
Edwin Arnold's The Rajpùt Nurse.
Browning's Hervé Riel.
Tennyson's The Revenge: A Battle of the Fleet.
Lanier's Revenge of Hamish.
Longfellow's The Wreck of the Hesperus.
Lowell's The Courtin'.
Whittier's Telling the Bees.

The methods of ballad-work in the class-room must
of course vary with the amount of time at disposal, the
extent of library privilege, the age and attainment of
the students, and, above all, the inclination of the
teacher.   For more ambitious topical study, queries will
readily suggest themselves as to the comparison between
the English ballads and the Scotch and Irish; between
our British ballads, as a whole, and the Scandinavian,

Teutonic, Romance, and Sclavonic; as to the nature of balladry in the Greek and Latin literatures; the character of popular song in the Orient, and the common Aryan stock of ballad material. Where the requisite books are at hand, it may be found a profitable exercise to commit a ballad to each student, who shall hunt down the various English versions, and, as far as his power reaches, the foreign equivalents. A wide field for investigation is afforded by the Robin Hood cycle of legendary lays; and it is of interest, too, to trace the deterioration of the Arthurian story.

But specific topical study can be put to advantage on the ballads themselves, the fifty collected here furnishing abundant data for discussion and illustration in regard to such subjects as the following : —

Ballad Language	{	Teutonic. Dialectic. Idiomatic.		
Ballad Music	{	Ballad Stanza	{	Description. Peculiar Fitness. Variations.
		Irregularities in	{	Metre. Accent. Rhyme.
		Significance of Irregularities.		
Ballad Structure	{	Introduction. Dramatic Element. Involution of Plot. Proportion of Ornament. Conclusion.		
Early English and Scottish Life as reflected in the Ballads	{	Government. Family. Employments. Pastimes. Manners.		

Early English and Scottish Character as Reflected in the Ballads { Aspirations. Principles. Tastes.

Democracy in the Ballads.

Nature in the Ballads.

Color in the Ballads.

History and Science in the Ballads.

Manhood in the Ballads.

Womanhood in the Ballads.

Childhood in the Ballads.

Standards of Morality in the Ballads.

Religion in the Ballads { Pagan Element — Christian Element { Catholic. Protestant.

Figures of Speech in the Ballads { Enumeration. General Character. Proportion.

Stock Material of the Ballads { Epithets. Numbers. Refrains. Stanzas. Situations.

Humor of the Ballads { In what consisting. At what directed.

Pathos of the Ballads { By what elicited. How expressed.

Ballads as a Revelation of Permanent English Characteristics.

Beauty of the Ballads { In Form. In Matter. In Spirit.

Truth of the Ballads { To Art. To Life.

A more delicate, difficult, and valuable variety of study
may be put upon the ballads, taken one by one, with
the aim of impressing upon a class the very simplicity
of strength and sweetness in this wild minstrelsy. The

mere recitation or reading of the ballad, with such unacademic and living comment as shall quicken the routine-cramped imagination of the average student to leap into a vivid realization of the swiftly shifted scenes, the listless sympathy to follow with eager comprehension the crowded, changing passions, the whole nature to thrill with the warm pulse of the rough old poem, is perhaps the surest way to drive the ballad home, trusting it to work within the student toward that spirit-development which is more truly the end of education than mental storage. For these primitive folk-songs which have done so much to educate the poetic sense in the fine peasantry of Scotland, — that peasantry which has produced an Ayrshire Ploughman and an Ettrick Shepherd, — are assuredly,

"Thanks to the human heart by which we live,"

among the best educators that can be brought into our schoolrooms.

BALLADS OF SUPERSTITION.

BALLADS OF SUPERSTITION.

THE WEE WEE MAN.

As I was wa'king all alane,
  Between a water and a wa',
There I spy'd a wee wee man,
  And he was the least that e'er I saw.

His legs were scant a shathmont's length,
  And sma' and limber was his thie,
Between his e'en there was a span,
  And between his shoulders there was three.

He took up a meikle stane,
  And he flang't as far as I could see;
Though I had been a Wallace wight,
  I couldna liften't to my knee.

"O wee wee man, but thou be strang!
  O tell me where thy dwelling be?"
"My dwelling's down at yon bonny bower;
  O will you go with me and see?"

On we lap, and awa' we rade,
  Till we cam' to yon bonny green;
We lighted down for to bait our horse,
  And out there cam' a lady sheen.

Four and twenty at her back,
    And they were a' clad out in green,
Though the King o' Scotland had been there,
    The warst o' them might hae been his Queen.

On we lap, and awa' we rade,
    Till we cam' to yon bonny ha',
Where the roof was o' the beaten gowd,
    And the floor was o' the crystal a'.

When we cam' to the stair foot,
    Ladies were dancing, jimp and sma';
But in the twinkling of an e'e,
    My wee wee man was clean awa'.

TAMLANE.

"O I FORBID ye, maidens a',
    That bind in snood your hair,
To come or gae by Carterhaugh,
    For young Tamlane is there."

Fair Janet sat within her bower,
    Sewing her silken seam,
And fain would be at Carterhaugh,
    Amang the leaves sae green.

She let the seam fa' to her foot,
   The needle to her tae,
And she's awa' to Carterhaugh,
   As quickly as she may.

She's prink'd hersell, and preen'd hersell,
   By the ae light o' the moon,
And she's awa to Carterhaugh,
   As fast as she could gang.

She hadna pu'd a red red rose,
   A rose but barely three,
When up and starts the young Tamlane,
   Says, " Lady, let a-be !

" What gars ye pu' the rose, Janet ?
   What gars ye break the tree ?
Or why come ye to Carterhaugh,
   Without the leave o' me ? "

" O I will pu' the flowers," she said,
   " And I will break the tree ;
And I will come to Carterhaugh,
   And ask na leave of thee."

But when she cam' to her father's ha',
   She looked sae wan and pale,
They thought the lady had gotten a fright,
   Or with sickness sair did ail.

Janet has kilted her green kirtle
 A little aboon her knee,
And she has snooded her yellow hair
 A little aboon her bree,
And she's awa to Carterhaugh,
 As fast as she can hie.

She hadna pu'd a rose, a rose,
 A rose but barely twae,
When up there started young Tamlane,
 Says, " Lady, thou pu's nae mae."

" Now ye maun tell the truth," she said,
 A word ye maunna lie;
O, were ye ever in haly chapel,
 Or sained in Christentie ? "

" The truth I'll tell to thee, Janet,
 A word I winna lie;
I was ta'en to the good church-door,
 And sained as well as thee.

" Randolph, Earl Murray, was my sire,
 Dunbar, Earl March, was thine;
We loved when we were children small,
 Which yet you well may mind.

" When I was a boy just turned of nine,
 My uncle sent for me,
To hunt, and hawk, and ride with him,
 And keep him companie.

" There came a wind out of the north,
 A sharp wind and a snell,
And a dead sleep came over me,
 And frae my horse I fell;
The Queen of Fairies she was there,
 And took me to hersell.

" And we, that live in Fairy-land,
 Nae sickness know nor pain;
I quit my body when I will,
 And take to it again.

" I quit my body when I please,
 Or unto it repair;
We can inhabit at our ease
 In either earth or air.

" Our shapes and size we can convert
 To either large or small;
An old nut-shell's the same to us
 As is the lofty hall.

" We sleep in rose-buds soft and sweet,
 We revel in the stream;
We wanton lightly on the wind,
 Or glide on a sunbeam.

" And never would I tire, Janet,
 In fairy-land to dwell;
But aye, at every seven years,
 They pay the teind to hell;
And I'm sae fat and fair of flesh,
 I fear 'twill be mysell!

" The morn at e'en is Hallowe'en ;
 Our fairy court will ride,
Through England and through Scotland baith,
 And through the warld sae wide,
And if that ye wad borrow me,
 At Miles Cross ye maun bide.

" And ye maun gae to the Miles Cross,
 Between twelve hours and one,
Tak' haly water in your hand,
 And cast a compass roun'."

" But how shall I thee ken, Tamlane,
 And how shall I thee knaw,
Amang the throng o' fairy folk,
 The like I never saw ? "

" The first court that comes alang,
 Ye'll let them a' pass by ;
The neist court that comes alang
 Salute them reverently.

" The third court that comes alang
 Is clad in robes o' green,
And it's the head court of them a',
 And in it rides the Queen.

" And I upon a milk-white steed,
 Wi' a gold star in my croun ;
Because I am a christen'd knight
 They give me that renoun.

" First let pass the black, Janet,
    And syne let pass the broun,
But grip ye to the milk-white steed,
    And pu' the rider doun.

" My right hand will be glov'd, Janet,
    My left hand will be bare,
And thae's the tokens I gie thee;
    Nae doubt I will be there.

" Ye'll seize upon me with a spring,
    And to the ground I'll fa',
And then you'll hear an elrish cry
    That Tamlane is awa'.

" They'll turn me in your arms, Janet,
    An adder and a snake;
But haud me fast, let me not pass,
    Gin ye would be my maik.

" They'll turn me in your arms, Janet,
    An adder and an aske;
They'll turn me in your arms, Janet,
    A bale that burns fast.

" They'll shape me in your arms, Janet,
    A dove, but and a swan:
And last they'll shape me in your arms
    A mother-naked man:
Cast your green mantle over me —
    And sae shall I be wan!"

Gloomy, gloomy was the night,
  And eerie was the way,
As fair Janet, in her green mantle,
  To Miles Cross she did gae.

About the dead hour o' the night
  She heard the bridles ring,
And Janet was as glad o' that
  As ony earthly thing.

There's haly water in her hand,
  She casts a compass round;
And straight she sees a fairy band
  Come riding o'er the mound.

And first gaed by the black, black steed,
  And then gaed by the broun;
But fast she gript the milk-white steed,
  And pu'd the rider doun.

She pu'd him frae the milk-white steed,
  And loot the bridle fa';
And up there raise an elrish cry;
  "He's won amang us a'!"

They shaped him in fair Janet's arms
  An aske, but and an adder;
She held him fast in every shape,
  To be her ain true lover.

They shaped him in her arms at last
    A mother-naked man,
She cuist her mantle over him,
    And sae her true love wan.

Up then spake the Queen o' Fairies,
    Out of a bush o' broom:
" She that has borrowed young Tamlane,
    Has gotten a stately groom!"

Up then spake the Queen o' Fairies,
    Out of a bush of rye:
" She's ta'en away the bonniest knight
    In a' my companie!

" But had I kenned, Tamlane," she says,
    " A lady wad borrow thee,
I wad hae ta'en out thy twa gray e'en,
    Put in twa e'en o' tree!

" Had I but kenned, Tamlane," she says,
    " Before ye came frae hame,
I wad hae ta'en out your heart of flesh,
    Put in a heart o' stane!

" Had I but had the wit yestreen
    That I hae coft this day,
I'd hae paid my teind seven times to hell,
    Ere you'd been won away!"

TRUE THOMAS.

True Thomas lay on Huntlie bank;
   A ferlie he spied with his e'e;
And there he saw a ladye bright,
   Come riding down by the Eildon tree.

Her skirt was o' the grass-green silk,
   Her mantle o' the velvet fine,
At ilka tett of her horse's mane,
   Hung fifty siller bells and nine.

True Thomas he pu'd aff his cap,
   And louted low down to his knee;
"All hail, thou mighty Queen of Heaven!
   For thy peer on earth I never did see."

"O no, O no, Thomas," she said,
   "That name does not belang to me;
I'm but the Queen of fair Elfland,
   That hither am come to visit thee!

"Harp and carp, Thomas," she said,
   "Harp and carp alang wi' me;
And if ye daur to kiss my lips,
   Sure of your bodie I shall be!"

"Betide me weal, betide me woe,
　　That weird shall never daunton me!"
　Syne he has kissed her rosy lips,
　　All underneath the Eildon tree.

"Now ye maun go wi' me," she said,
　　"True Thomas, ye maun go wi' me;
　And ye maun serve me seven years,
　　Through weal or woe as may chance to be."

　She's mounted on her milk-white steed,
　　She's ta'en True Thomas up behind;
　And aye, whene'er her bridle rang,
　　The steed gaed swifter than the wind.

　O they rade on, and further on,
　　The steed gaed swifter than the wind;
　Until they reached a desert wide,
　　And living land was left behind.

"Light down, light down now, Thomas," she said,
　　"And lean your head upon my knee;
　Light down, and rest a little space,
　　And I will show you ferlies three.

"O see ye na that braid braid road,
　　That stretches o'er the lily leven?
　That is the path of wickedness,
　　Though some call it the road to heaven.

" And see ye na yon narrow road,
　　Sae thick beset wi' thorns and briers ?
That is the path of righteousness,
　　Though after it but few enquires.

" And see ye na yon bonny road,
　　That winds about the ferny brae ?
That is the way to fair Elfland,
　　Where you and I this night maun gae.

" But, Thomas, ye maun hauld your tongue,
　　Whatever you may hear or see ;
For if ye speak word in Elfin land,
　　Ye'll ne'er win back to your ain countrie ! "

O they rade on, and further on,
　　And they waded through rivers aboon the knee,
And they saw neither sun nor moon,
　　But they heard the roaring of a sea.

It was mirk mirk night, there was nae stern-light,
　　And they waded through red blude to the knee ;
For a' the blude that's shed on earth,
　　Rins through the springs o' that countrie.

Syne they came to a garden green,
　　And she pu'd an apple frae a tree —
" Take this for thy wages, True Thomas ;
　　It will give thee the tongue that can never lie ! "

"My tongue is my ain!" True Thomas he said,
 "A gudely gift ye wad gie to me!
I neither dought to buy nor sell,
 At fair or tryste where I may be.

"I dought neither speak to prince nor peer,
 Nor ask for grace from fair ladye!"
"Now hauld thy tongue, Thomas!" she said
 "For as I say, so must it be."

He has gotten a coat of the even claith,
 And a pair o' shoon of the velvet green;
And till seven years were come and gane,
 True Thomas on earth was never seen.

THE ELFIN KNIGHT.

The Elfin knight stands on yon hill;
 (Blaw, blaw, blaw winds, blaw,)
Blawing his horn baith loud and shrill,
 (And the wind has blawn my plaid awa'.)

"If I had the horn that I hear blawn,
 (Blaw, blaw, blaw winds, blaw,)
And the bonnie knight that blaws the horn!"
 (And the wind has blawn my plaid awa'.)

She had na sooner thae words said ;
   (Blaw, blaw, blaw winds, blaw,)
Than the Elfin knight cam' to her side :
   (And the wind has blawn my plaid awa'.)

"Thou art too young a maid," quoth he,
   (Blaw, blaw, blaw winds, blaw,)
"Married wi' me you ill wad be."
   (And the wind has blawn my plaid awa'.)

"I hae a sister younger than me ;
   (Blaw, blaw, blaw winds, blaw,)
And she was married yesterday."
   (And the wind has blawn my plaid awa'.)

"Married to me ye shall be nane ;
   (Blaw, blaw, blaw winds, blaw,)
Till ye mak' me a sark without a seam ;
   (And the wind has blawn my plaid awa'.)

"And ye maun shape it, knifeless, sheerless,
   (Blaw, blaw, blaw winds, blaw,)
And ye maun sew it, needle-threedless ;
   (And the wind has blawn my plaid awa'.)

"And ye maun wash it within a well,
   (Blaw, blaw, blaw winds, blaw,)
Whaur dew never wat, nor rain ever fell,
   (And the wind has blawn my plaid awa'.)

"And ye maun dry it upon a thorn,
(Blaw, blaw, blaw winds, blaw,)
That never budded sin' Adam was born."
(And the wind has blawn my plaid awa'.)

"O gin that kindness I do for thee;
(Blaw, blaw, blaw winds, blaw,)
There's something ye maun do for me.
(And the wind has blawn my plaid awa'.)

"I hae an acre o' gude lea-land,
(Blaw, blaw, blaw winds, blaw,)
Between the saut sea and the strand;
(And the wind has blawn my plaid awa'.)

"Ye'll plough it wi' your blawing horn,
(Blaw, blaw, blaw winds, blaw,)
And ye will sow it wi' pepper corn,
(And the wind has blawn my plaid awa'.)

"And ye maun harrow't wi' a single tyne,
(Blaw, blaw, blaw winds, blaw,)
And shear it wi' a sheep's shank bane;
(And the wind has blawn my plaid awa'.)

"And bigg a cart o' lime and stane,
(Blaw, blaw, blaw winds, blaw,)
And Robin Redbreast maun trail it hame,
(And the wind has blawn my plaid awa'.)

"And ye maun barn it in a mouse-hole,
    (Blaw, blaw, blaw winds, blaw,)
And ye maun thresh it in your shoe sole;
    (And the wind has blawn my plaid awa'.)

"And ye maun winnow it wi' your loof,
    (Blaw, blaw, blaw winds, blaw,)
And ye maun sack it in your glove;
    (And the wind has blawn my plaid awa'.)

"And ye maun dry it, but candle or coal,
    (Blaw, blaw, blaw winds, blaw,)
And ye maun grind it, but quern or mill;
    (And the wind has blawn my plaid awa'.)

"When ye hae done, and finish'd your wark,
    (Blaw, blaw, blaw winds, blaw,)
Then come to me, and ye'se get your sark!"
    (And the wind has blawn my plaid awa'.)

LADY ISOBEL AND THE ELF-KNIGHT.

THERE cam' a bird out o' a bush,
    On water for to dine,
An' sighing sair, says the king's daughter,
    "O wae's this heart o' mine!"

He's taen a harp into his hand,
    He's harped them all asleep,
Except it was the king's daughter,
    Who ae wink couldna get.

He's luppen on his berry-brown steed,
    Taen 'er on behind himsell,
Then baith rede down to that water
    That they ca' Wearie's Well.

"Wide in, wide in, my lady fair,
    Nae harm shall thee befall ;
Aft times hae I water'd my steed
    Wi' the water o' Wearie's Well."

The first step that she stepped in,
    She stepped to the knee ;
And sighing sair, says this lady fair,
    "This water's nae for me."

"Wide in, wide in, my lady fair,
    Nae harm shall thee befall ;
Aft times hae I water'd my steed
    Wi' the water o' Wearie's Well."

The neist step that she stepped in,
    She stepped to the middle ;
"O," sighend says this lady fair,
    "I've wat my gowden girdle."

"Wide in, wide in, my lady fair,
    Nae harm shall thee befall ;
Aft times hae I water'd my steed
    Wi' the water o' Wearie's Well."

The neist step that she stepped in,
    She stepped to the chin ;
" O," sighend says this lady fair,
    " I'll wade nae farer in."

" Seven king's-daughters I've drownd here,
    In the water o' Wearie's Well,
And I'll mak' you the eight o' them,
    And ring the common bell."

" Sin' I am standing here," she says,
    " This dowie death to die,
Ae kiss o' your comely mouth
    I'm sure wad comfort me."

He's louted him o'er his saddle bow,
    To kiss her cheek and chin ;
She's taen him in her arms twa,
    An' thrown him headlong in.

" Sin' seven king's-daughters ye've drownd here,
    In the water o' Wearie's Well,
I'll mak' you bridegroom to them a',
    An' ring the bell mysell."

TOM THUMBE.

In Arthurs court Tom Thumbe did live,
   A man of mickle might,
The best of all the table round,
   And eke a doughty knight:

His stature but an inch in height,
   Or quarter of a span;
Then thinke you not this little knight,
   Was prov'd a valiant man?

His father was a plow-man plaine,
   His mother milkt the cow,
But yet the way to get a sonne
   This couple knew not how,

Untill such time this good old man
   To learned Merlin goes,
And there to him his deepe desires
   In secret manner showes,

How in his heart he wisht to have
   A childe, in time to come,
To be his heire, though it might be
   No bigger than his Thumbe.

Of which old Merlin thus foretold,
   That he his wish should have,
And so this sonne of stature small
   The charmer to him gave.

No blood nor bones in him should be,
   In shape and being such,
That men should heare him speake, but not
   His wandring shadow touch :

But all unseene to goe or come
   Whereas it pleasd him still ;
And thus King Arthurs Dwarfe was born,
   To fit his fathers will :

And in foure minutes grew so fast,
   That he became so tall
As was the plowmans thumbe in height,
   And so they did him call

Tom Thumbe, the which the Fayry-Queene
   There gave him to his name,
Who, with her traine of Goblins grim,
   Unto his christning came.

Whereas she cloath'd him richly brave,
   In garments fine and faire,
Which lasted him for many yeares
   In seemely sort to weare.

His hat made of an oaken leafe,
   His shirt a spiders web,
Both light and soft for those his limbes
   That were so smally bred;

His hose and doublet thistle downe,
   Togeather weav'd full fine;
His stockins of an apple greene,
   Made of the outward rine;

His garters were two little haires,
   Pull'd from his mothers eye,
His bootes and shooes a mouses skin,
   There tand most curiously.

Thus, like a lustie gallant, he
   Adventured forth to goe,
With other children in the streets
   His pretty trickes to show.

Where he for counters, pinns, and points,
   And cherry stones did play,
Till he amongst those gamesters young
   Had loste his stocke away,

Yet could he soone renew the same,
   When as most nimbly he
Would dive into their cherry-baggs,
   And there partaker be,

Unseene or felt by any one,
  Untill a scholler shut
This nimble youth into a boxe,
  Wherein his pins he put.

Of whom to be reveng'd, he tooke
  (In mirth and pleasant game)
Black pots, and glasses, which he hung
  Upon a bright sunne-beam.

The other boyes to doe the like,
  In pieces broke them quite;
For which they were most soundly whipt,
  Whereat he laught outright.

And so Tom Thumbe restrained was
  From these his sports and play,
And by his mother after that
  Compel'd at home to stay.

Whereas about a Christmas time,
  His father a hog had kil'd,
And Tom would see the puddings made,
  For fear they should be spil'd.

He sate upon the pudding-boule,
  The candle for to hold;
Of which there is unto this day
  A pretty pastime told:

For Tom fell in, and could not be
　　For ever after found,
For in the blood and batter he
　　Was strangely lost and drownd.

Where searching long, but all in vaine,
　　His mother after that
Into a pudding thrust her sonne,
　　Instead of minced fat.

Which pudding of the largest size.
　　Into the kettle throwne,
Made all the rest to fly thereout,
　　As with a whirle-wind blowne.

For so it tumbled up and downe.
　　Within the liquor there,
As if the devill had been boiled ;
　　Such was his mothers feare,

That up she took the pudding strait.
　　And gave it at the door
Unto a tinker, which from thence
　　In his blacke budget bore.

From which Tom Thumbe got loose at last
　　And home return'd againe :
Where he from following dangers long
　　In safety did remaine.

Now after this, in sowing time,
　　His father would him have
Into the field to drive his plow,
　　And thereupon him gave

A whip made of a barly straw
　　To drive the cattle on:
Where, in a furrow'd land new sowne,
　　Poore Tom was lost and gon.

Now by a raven of great strength
　　Away he thence was borne,
And carried in the carrions beake
　　Even like a graine of corne,

Unto a giants castle top,
　　In which he let him fall,
Where soone the giant swallowed up
　　His body, cloathes and all.

But in his stomach did Tom Thumbe
　　So great a rumbling make,
That neither day nor night he could
　　The smallest quiet take,

Untill the giant had him spewd
　　Three miles into the sea,
Whereas a fish soone tooke him up
　　And bore him thence away.

Which lusty fish was after caught
  And to king Arthur sent,
Where Tom was found, and made his dwarfe,
  Whereas his dayes he spent

Long time in lively jollity,
  Belov'd of all the court,
And none like Tom was then esteem'd
  Among the noble sort.

Amongst his deedes of courtship done,
  His highnesse did command,
That he should dance a galliard brave
  Upon his queenes left hand.

The which he did, and for the same
  The king his signet gave,
Which Tom about his middle wore
  Long time a girdle brave.

Now after this the king would not
  Abroad for pleasure goe,
But still Tom Thumbe must ride with him,
  Plac'd on his saddle-bow.

Where on a time when as it rain'd,
  Tom Thumbe most nimbly crept
In at a button hole, where he
  Within his bosome slept.

And being neere his highnesse heart,
  He crav'd a wealthy boone,
A liberall gift, the which the king
  Commanded to be done,

For to relieve his fathers wants,
  And mothers, being old;
Which was so much of silver coin
  As well his armes could hold.

And so away goes lusty Tom,
  With three pence on his backe,
A heavy burthen, which might make
  His wearied limbes to cracke.

So travelling two dayes and nights,
  With labour and great paine,
He came into the house whereas
  His parents did remaine;

Which was but halfe a mile in space
  From good king Arthurs court,
The which in eight and forty houres
  He went in weary sort.

But comming to his fathers doore,
  He there such entrance had   ·
As made his parents both rejoice,
  And he thereat was glad.

His mother in her apron tooke
   Her gentle sonne in haste,
And by the fier side, within
   A walnut shell, him plac'd:

Whereas they feasted him three dayes
   Upon a hazell nut,
Whereon he rioted so long
   He them to charges put;

And thereupon grew wonderous sicke,
   Through eating too much meate,
Which was sufficient for a month
   For this great man to eate.

But now his businesse call'd him foorth,
   King Arthurs court to see,
Whereas no longer from the same
   He could a stranger be.

But yet a few small April drops,
   Which settled in the way,
His long and weary journey forth
   Did hinder and so stay.

Until his carefull father tooke
   A hollow straw in sport,
And with one blast blew this his sonne
   Into king Arthurs court.

Now he with tilts and turnaments
   Was entertained so,
That all the best of Arthurs knights
   Did him much pleasure show.

As good Sir Lancelot of the Lake,
   Sir Tristram, and sir Guy ;
Yet none compar'd with brave Tom Thum,
   In knightly chivalry.

In honor of which noble day,
   And for his ladies sake,
A challenge in king Arthurs court
   Tom Thumbe did bravely make.

Gainst whom these noble knights did run,
   Sir Chinon and the rest,
Yet still Tom Thumbe with matchles might
   Did beare away the best.

He likewise cleft the smallest haire
   From his faire ladies head,
Not hurting her whose even hand
   Him lasting honors bred.

Such were his deeds and noble acts
   In Arthurs court there showne,
As like in all the world beside
   Was hardly seene or knowne.

Now at these sports he toyld himselfe
    That he a sicknesse tooke,
Through which all manly exercise
    He carelesly forsooke.

Where lying on his bed sore sicke,
    King Arthurs doctor came,
With cunning skill, by physicks art,
    To ease and cure the same.

His body being so slender small,
    This cunning doctor tooke
A fine prospective glasse, with which
    He did in secret looke

Into his sickened body downe,
    And therein saw that Death
Stood ready in his wasted guts
    To sease his vitall breath.

His armes and leggs consum'd as small
    As was a spiders web,
Through which his dying houre grew on,
    For all his limbes grew dead.

His face no bigger than an ants,
    Which hardly could be seene:
The losse of which renowned knight
    Much griev'd the king and queene.

And so with peace and quietnesse
    He left this earth below;
And up into the Fayry Land
    His ghost did fading goe.

Whereas the Fayry Queene receiv'd
    With heavy mourning cheere,
The body of this valiant knight
    Whom she esteem'd so deere.

For with her dancing nymphes in greene,
    She fetcht him from his bed,
With musicke and sweet melody
    So soone as life was fled:

For whom king Arthur and his knights
    Full forty daies did mourne;
And, in remembrance of his name
    That was so strangely borne,

He built a tomb of marble gray,
    And yeare by yeare did come
To celebrate the mournefull day,
    And buriall of Tom Thum.

Whose fame still lives in England here,
    Amongst the countrey sort;
Of whom our wives and children small
    Tell tales of pleasant sport.

KEMPION.

Her mither died when she was young,
  Which gave her cause to make great moan ;
Her father married the warse woman
  That ever lived in Christendom.

She served her well wi' foot and hand,
  In everything that she could dee ;
But her stepmither hated her warse and warse,
  And a powerful wicked witch was she.

"Come hither, come hither, ye cannot choose ;
  And lay your head low on my knee ;
The heaviest weird I will you read
  That ever was read to gay ladye.

"Mickle dolour sall ye dree
  When o'er the saut seas maun ye swim ;
And far mair dolour sall ye dree
  When up to Estmere Crags ye climb.

"I weird ye be a fiery snake ;
  And borrowed sall ye never be,
Till Kempion, the kingis son,
  Come to the crag and thrice kiss thee.
Until the warld comes to an end,
  Borrowed sall ye never be ! "

O mickle dolour did she dree,
   And aye the saut seas o'er she swam ;
And far mair dolour did she dree
   On Estmere Crags, when up she clamb.

And aye she cried on Kempion,
   Gin he would but come to her han' : —
Now word has gane to Kempion,
   That siccan a beast was in the lan'.

"Now by my sooth," said Kempion,
   "This fiery beast I'll gang and see."
"An' by my sooth," said Segramour,
   "My ae brither, I'll gang wi' thee."

They twa hae biggit a bonny boat,
   And they hae set her to the sea ;
But a mile afore they reach'd the shore,
   Around them 'gan the red fire flee.

The worm leapt out, the worm leapt down,
   She plaited nine times round stock and stane ;
And aye as the boat cam' to the beach,
   O she hae strickit it aff again.

"Min' how you steer, my brither dear :
   Keep further aff ! " said Segramour ;
"She'll drown us deep in the saut, saut sea,
   Or burn us sair, if we come on shore."

Syne Kempion has bent an arblast bow,
　And aimed an arrow at her head ;
And swore, if she didna quit the shore,
　Wi' that same shaft to shoot her dead.

" Out o' my stythe I winna rise,
　Nor quit my den for the fear o' thee,
Till Kempion, the kingis son,
　Come to the crag an' thrice kiss me."

He's louted him o'er the Estmere Crag,
　And he has gi'en that beast a kiss :
In she swang, and again she cam',
　And aye her speech was a wicked hiss.

" Out o' my stythe I winna rise,
　An' not for a' thy bow nor thee,
Till Kempion, the kingis son,
　Come to the crag an' thrice kiss me."

He's louted him o'er the Estmere Crag,
　And he has gi'en her kisses twa ;
In she swang, and again she cam',
　The fieriest beast that ever you saw.

" Out o' my stythe I winna rise,
　Nor quit my den for the fear o' thee,
Till Kempion, the kingis son,
　Come to the crag an' thrice kiss me."

He's louted him o'er the lofty crag,
    And he has gi'en her kisses three;
In she swang, a loathly worm;
    An' out she stepped, a fair ladye.

Nae cleeding had this lady fair,
    To keep her body frae the cold;
But Kempion took his mantle aff,
    And around his ain true love did fold.

"An' by my sooth," says Kempion,
    "My ain true love! — for this is she, —
They surely had a heart o' stane,
    Could put thee to this misery.

"O was it wer-wolf in the wood,
    Or was it mermaid in the sea,
Or wicked man, or wile woman,
    My ain true love, that mis-shaped thee?"

"It was na wer-wolf in the wood,
    Nor was it mermaid in the sea;
But it was my wicked stepmither,
    And wae and weary may she be!"

O a heavier weird light her upon
    Than ever fell on wile woman!
Her hair sall grow rough, an' her teeth grow lang,
    An' aye upon four feet maun she gang."

ALISON GROSS.

O ALISON GROSS, that lives in yon tower,
   The ugliest witch in the north countrie,
Has trysted me ae day up till her bower,
   And mony fair speech she made to me.

She straiked my head, and she kaim'd my hair,
   And she set me down saftly on her knee;
Says, "Gin ye will be my lemman sae true,
   Sae mony braw things as I wad you gie."

She shaw'd me a mantle o' red scarlet,
   Wi' gowden flowers and fringes fine;
Says, "Gin ye will be my lemman sae true,
   This gudely gift it sall be thine."

"Awa', awa', ye ugly witch!
   Haud far awa', and lat me be;
I never will be your lemman sae true,
   And I wish I were out o' your companie."

She neist brocht a sark o' the saftest silk,
   Weel wrought wi' pearls about the band;
Says, "Gin ye will be my ain true-love,
   This gudely gift ye sall command."

She shaw'd me a cup o' the gude red gowd,
    Weel set wi' jewels sae fair to see;
Says, "Gin ye will be my lemman sae true,
    This gudely gift I will you gie."

"Awa', awa', ye ugly witch!
    Haud far awa', and lat me be;
For I wadna ance kiss your ugly mouth
    For a' the gifts that you could gie."

She's turn'd her richt and round about,
    And thrice she blew on a grass-green horn;
And she sware by the moon, and the stars aboon,
    That she'd gar me rue the day I was born.

Then out she has ta'en a silver wand,
    And she's turn'd her three times round and round;
She's muttered sic words, that my strength it fail'd,
    And I fell down senseless on the ground.

She's turned me into an ugly worm,
    And gar'd me toddle about the tree;
And ay, on ilka Saturday's night,
    Auld Alison Gross, she cam' to me,

Wi' silver basin, and silver kaim,
    To kaim my headie upon her knee;
But or I had kiss'd her ugly mouth,
    I'd rather hae toddled about the tree.

But as it fell out on last Hallowe'en,
   When the Seely Court was ridin' by,
The Queen lighted down on a gowan bank,
   Nae far frae the tree where I wont to lye.

She took me up in her milk-white hand,
   And she straiked me three times o'er her knee ;
She changed me again to my ain proper shape,
   And I nae mair maun toddle about the tree.

———————

THE WIFE OF USHER'S WELL.

There lived a wife at Usher's Well,
   And a wealthy wife was she ;
She had three stout and stalwart sons,
   And sent them o'er the sea.

They hadna been a week from her,
   A week but barely ane,
When word cam' to the carline wife,
   That her three sons were gane.

They hadna been a week from her,
   A week but barely three,
When word cam' to the carline wife,
   That her sons she'd never see.

"I wish the wind may never cease,
　　Nor fashes in the flood,
Till my three sons come hame to me,
　　In earthly flesh and blood !"

It fell about the Martinmas,
　　When nights are lang and mirk,
The carline wife's three sons cam' hame,
　　And their hats were o' the birk.

It neither grew in syke nor ditch,
　　Nor yet in ony sheugh ;
But at the gates o' Paradise,
　　That birk grew fair eneugh.

"Blow up the fire, now, maidens mine,
　　Bring water from the well !
For a' my house shall feast this night,
　　Sin' my three sons are well."

And she has made to them a bed,
　　She's made it large and wide ;
And she's happed her mantle them about,
　　Sat down at the bed-side.

Up then crew the red red cock,
　　And up and crew the gray ;
The eldest to the youngest said,
　　" 'Tis time we were away."

"The cock doth craw, the day doth daw,
    The channerin' worm doth chide;
  Gin we be miss'd out o' our place,
    A sair pain we maun bide."

"Lie still, lie still a little wee while,
    Lie still but if we may;
  Gin my mother should miss us when she wakes,
    She'll go mad ere it be day."

  O it's they've ta'en up their mother's mantle,
    And they've hangd it on the pin:
"O lang may ye hing, my mother's mantle,
    Ere ye hap us again!

'Fare-ye-weel, my mother dear!
    Fareweel to barn and byre!
  And fare-ye-weel, the bonny lass,
    That kindles my mother's fire."

A LYKE-WAKE DIRGE.

THIS ae nighte, this ae nighte,
    Everie nighte and alle,
Fire, and sleete, and candle-lighte,
    And Christe receive thye saule.

When thou from hence away art paste,
    Everie nighte and alle,
To Whinny-muir thou comest at laste,
    And Christe receive thye saule.

If ever thou gavest hosen and shoon,
   Everie nighte and alle,
Sit thee down and put them on,
   And Christe receive thye saule.

If hosen and shoon thou ne'er gav'st nane,
   Everie nighte and alle,
The whinnes shall pricke thee to the bare bane,
   And Christe receive thye saule.

From Whinny-muir when thou mayst passe,
   Everie nighte and alle,
To Brigg o' Dread thou comest at last,
   And Christe receive thye saule.

From Brigg o' Dread when thou mayst passe,
   Everie nighte and alle,
To Purgatory Fire thou comest at last,
   And Christe receive thye saule.

If ever thou gavest meate or drinke,
   Everie nighte and alle,
The fire shall never make thee shrinke,
   And Christe receive thye saule.

If meate or drinke thou ne'er gav'st nane,
   Everie nighte and alle,
The fire will burne thee to the bare bane,
   And Christe receive thye saule.

This ae nighte, this ae nighte,
    Everie nighte and alle,
Fire, and sleete, and candle-lighte,
    And Christe receive thye saule.

PROUD LADY MARGARET.

'Twas on a night, an evening bright,
    When the dew began to fa',
Lady Margaret was walkin' up and doun,
    Looking ower the castle wa'.

She lookit east, she lookit west,
    To see what she could spy,
When a gallant knight cam' in her sight,
    And to the gate drew nigh.

" God mak' you safe and free, fair maid,
    God mak' you safe and free ! "
" O sae fa' you, ye stranger knight,
    What is your will wi' me ? "

" It's I am come to this castle,
    To seek the love o' thee ;
And if ye grant me not your love
    All for your sake I'll die."

" If ye should die for me, young man,
 There's few for ye will maen;
For mony a better has died for me,
 Whose graves are growing green."

" O winna ye pity me, fair maid,
 O winna ye pity me?
Hae pity for a courteous knight,
 Whose love is laid on thee."

" Ye say ye are a courteous knight,
 But I misdoubt ye sair;
I think ye're but a miller lad,
 By the white clothes ye wear.

" But ye maun read my riddle," she said,
 " And answer me questions three;
And but ye read them richt," she said,
 " Gae stretch ye out and die.

" What is the fairest flower, tell me,
 That grows on muir or dale?
And what is the bird, the bonnie bird,
 Sings next the nightingale?
And what is the finest thing," she says,
 " That king or queen can wale?"

" The primrose is the fairest flower,
 That springs on muir or dale;

The mavis is the sweetest bird
 Next to the nightingale;
And yellow gowd's the finest thing,
 That king or queen can wale."

" But what is the little coin," she said,
 " Wad buy my castle boun'?
And what's the little boat," she said,
 " Can sail the warld all roun'?"

" O hey, how mony small pennies
 Mak' thrice three thousand poun'?
O hey, how mony small fishes
 Swim a' the saut sea roun'?"

' I think ye are my match," she said,
 " My match, an' something mair;
Ye are the first ere got the grant
 Of love frae my father's heir.

" My father was lord o' nine castles,
 My mither lady o' three;
My father was lord o' nine castles,
 And there's nane to heir but me,
Unless it be Willie, my ae brither,
 But he's far ayont the sea."

" If your father's lord o' nine castles,
 Your mither lady o' three;
It's I am Willie, your ae brither,
 Was far ayont the sea."

" If ye be my brither Willie," she said,
   " As I doubt sair ye be,
This nicht I'll neither eat nor drink,
   But gae alang wi' thee."

" Ye've owre ill-washen feet, Margaret,
   And owre ill-washen hands,
And owre coarse robes on your body,
   Alang wi' me to gang.

" The worms they are my bedfellows,
   And the cauld clay my sheet,
And the higher that the wind does blaw,
   The sounder do I sleep.

" My body's buried in Dunfermline,
   Sae far ayont the sea:
But day nor night nae rest can I get,
   A' for the pride of thee.

" Leave aff your pride, Margaret," he says ;
   " Use it not ony mair,
Or, when ye come where I hae been,
   Ye will repent it sair.

" Cast aff, cast aff, sister," he says,
   " The gowd band frae your croun;
For if ye gang where I hae been,
   Ye'll wear it laigher doun.

" When ye are in the gude kirk set,
    The gowd pins in your hair,
  Ye tak' mair delight in your feckless dress,
    Than in your mornin' prayer.

" And when ye walk in the kirkyard,
    And in your dress are seen,
  There is nae lady that spies your face,
    But wishes your grave were green.

" Ye're straight and tall, handsome withal,
    But your pride owergangs your wit;
  If ye do not your ways refrain,
    In Pirie's chair ye'll sit.

" In Pirie's chair ye'll sit, I say,
    The lowest seat in hell;
  If ye do not amend your ways,
    It's there that ye maun dwell!"

  Wi' that he vanished frae her sight,
    In the twinking of an eye;
  And naething mair the lady saw
    But the gloomy clouds and sky.

THE TWA SISTERS O' BINNORIE.

THERE were twa sisters lived in a bower;
    Binnorie, O Binnorie;
The youngest o' them, O she was a flower,
    By the bonnie mill-dams o' Binnorie.

There cam' a squire frae the west,
    Binnorie, O Binnorie;
He lo'ed them baith, but the youngest best,
    By the bonnie mill-dams o' Binnorie.

He courted the eldest wi' glove and ring,
    Binnorie, O Binnorie;
But he lo'ed the youngest abune a' thing,
    By the bonnie mill-dams o' Binnorie.

The eldest she was vexed sair,
    Binnorie, O Binnorie;
And sore envied her sister fair,
    By the bonnie mill-dams o' Binnorie.

The eldest said to the youngest ane,
    Binnorie, O Binnorie;
" Will ye see our father's ships come in ? "
    By the bonnie mill-dams o' Binnorie.

She's ta'en her by the lily hand;
   Binnorie, O Binnorie;
And led her down to the river strand,
   By the bonnie mill-dams o' Binnorie.

The youngest stood upon a stane;
   Binnorie, O Binnorie;
The eldest cam' and pushed her in,
   By the bonnie mill-dams o' Binnorie

" O sister, sister, reach your hand,
   Binnorie, O Binnorie;
And ye shall be heir of half my land,"
   By the bonnie mill-dams o' Binnorie.

" O sister, I'll not reach my hand,
   Binnorie, O Binnorie;
And I'll be the heir of all your land;
   By the bonnie mill-dams o' Binnorie.

" Shame fa' the hand that I should take,
   Binnorie, O Binnorie;
It has twined me and my world's make;"
   By the bonnie mill-dams o' Binnorie.

" O sister, sister, reach your glove,
   Binnorie, O Binnorie;
And sweet William shall be your love;"
   By the bonnie mill-dams o' Binnorie.

" Sink on, nor hope for hand or glove,
    Binnorie, O Binnorie ;
And sweet William shall be mair my love,
    By the bonnie mill-dams o' Binnorie.

" Your cherry cheeks, and your yellow hair,
    Binnorie, O Binnorie ;
Had gar'd me gang maiden ever mair,"
    By the bonnie mill-dams o' Binnorie.

Sometimes she sank, and sometimes she swam,
    Binnorie, O Binnorie ;
Until she cam' to the miller's dam ;
    By the bonnie mill-dams o' Binnorie.

The miller's daughter was baking bread,
    Binnorie, O Binnorie ;
And gaed for water as she had need,
    By the bonnie mill-dams o' Binnorie.

" O father, father, draw your dam !
    Binnorie, O Binnorie ;
For there is a lady or milk-white swan,"
    By the bonnie mill-dams o' Binnorie.

The miller hasted and drew his dam,
    Binnorie, O Binnorie ;
And there he found a drown'd woman,
    By the bonnie mill-dams o' Binnorie.

Ye couldna see her yellow hair,
   Binnorie, O Binnorie;
For gowd and pearls that were sae rare;
   By the bonnie mill-dams o' Binnorie.

Ye couldna see her middle sma',
   Binnorie, O Binnorie;
Her gowden girdle was sae braw,
   By the bonnie mill-dams o' Binnorie.

Ye couldna see her lilie feet,
   Binnorie, O Binnorie;
Her gowden fringes were sae deep,
   By the bonnie mill-dams o' Binnorie.

" Sair will they be, whae'er they be,
   Binnorie, O Binnorie;
The hearts that live to weep for thee!"
   By the bonnie mill-dams o' Binnorie.

There cam' a harper passing by,
   Binnorie, O Binnorie;
The sweet pale face he chanced to spy,
   By the bonnie mill-dams o' Binnorie.

And when he looked that lady on,
   Binnorie, O Binnorie;
He sighed and made a heavy moan,
   By the bonnie mill-dams o' Binnorie.

He has ta'en three locks o' her yellow hair,
　　Binnorie, O Binnorie;
And wi' them strung his harp sae rare,
　　By the bonnie mill-dams o' Binnorie.

He brought the harp to her father's hall;
　　Binnorie, O Binnorie;
And there was the court assembled all;
　　By the bonnie mill-dams o' Binnorie

He set the harp upon a stane,
　　Binnorie, O Binnorie;
And it began to play alane,
　　By the bonnie mill-dams o' Binnorie.

And sune the harp sang loud and clear,
　　Binnorie, O Binnorie!
"Farewell, my father and mither dear!"
　　By the bonnie mill-dams o' Binnorie

And neist when the harp began to sing,
　　Binnorie, O Binnorie!
'Twas "Farewell, sweetheart!" said the string,
　　By the bonnie mill-dams o' Binnorie.

And then as plain as plain could be,
　　Binnorie, O Binnorie!
"There sits my sister wha drownèd me!"
　　By the bonnie mill-dams o' Binnorie.

THE DEMON LOVER.

"O, WHERE hae ye been, my lang-lost love,
    This lang seven years an' more ? "
"O, I'm come to seek my former vows
    Ye granted me before."

"O, haud your tongue o' your former vows,
    For they'll breed bitter strife ;
  O, haud your tongue o' your former vows,
    For I am become a wife."

  He turned him right an' round about,
    And the tear blinded his e'e ;
"I wad never hae trodden on Irish ground
    If it hadna been for thee.

"I might hae had a king's daughter
    Far, far ayont the sea,
  I might hae had a king's daughter,
    Had it nae been for love o' thee."

"If ye might hae had a king's daughter,
    Yoursel' ye hae to blame ;
  Ye might hae taken the king's daughter,
    For ye kenn'd that I was nane."

"O fause be the vows o' womankind,
  But fair is their fause bodie;
I wad never hae trodden on Irish ground
  Had it nae been for love o' thee."

"If I was to leave my husband dear,
  And my twa babes also,
O where is it ye would tak' me to,
  If I with thee should go?"

"I hae seven ships upon the sea,
  The eighth brouct me to land,
Wi' four-and-twenty bold mariners,
  And music of ilka hand."

She has taken up her twa little babes,
  Kiss'd them baith cheek and chin;
"O fare ye weel, my ain twa babes,
  For I'll never see you again."

She set her foot upon the ship,
  No mariners could she behold;
But the sails were o' the taffetie,
  And the masts o' the beaten gold.

"O how do you love the ship?" he said,
  "O how do you love the sea?
And how do you love the bold mariners
  That wait upon thee and me?"

"O I do love the ship," she said,
     "And I do love the sea;
But wae to the dim mariners
     That naewhere I can see!"

They hadna sailed a league, a league,
     A league but barely three,
When dismal grew his countenance,
     And drumly grew his e'e.

The masts that were like the beaten gold,
     Bent not on the heaving seas;
The sails that were o' the taffetie
     Fill'd not in the east land breeze.

They hadna sailed a league, a league,
     A league but barely three,
Until she espied his cloven hoof,
     And she wept right bitterlie.

"O haud your tongue o' your weeping," he says:
     "O' your weeping now let me be;
I will show you how the lilies grow
     On the banks of Italy."

"O what hills are yon, yon pleasant hills,
     That the sun shines sweetly on?"
"O yon are the hills o' heaven," he said,
     "Where you will never won."

"O what'n a mountain's yon," she said,
　"Sae dreary wi' frost an' snow?"
O yon is the mountain o' hell," he cried,
　"Where you and I maun go!"

And aye when she turn'd her round about,
　Aye taller he seemed for to be;
Until that the tops o' that gallant ship
　Nae taller were than he.

He strack the tapmast wi' his hand,
　The foremast wi' his knee;
And he brak that gallant ship in twain,
　And sank her i' the sea.

———

RIDDLES WISELY EXPOUNDED.

THERE was a knicht riding frae the east,
　Jennifer gentle an' rosemaree.
Who had been wooing at monie a place,
　As the dew flies ower the mulberry tree.

He cam' unto a widow's door,
And speird whare her three dochters were.

The auldest ane's to a washing gane,
The second's to a baking gane.

The youngest ane's to a wedding gane,
And it will be nicht or she be hame.

He sat him doun upon a stane,
Till thir three lasses cam' tripping hame.

The auldest ane she let him in,
And pin'd the door wi' a siller pin.

The second ane she made his bed,
And laid saft pillows unto his head.

The youngest ane was bauld and bricht,
And she tarried for words wi' this unco knicht.

" Gin ye will answer me questions ten,
The morn ye sall be made my ain.

" O what is heigher nor the tree?
And what is deeper nor the sea?

" Or what is heavier nor the lead?
And what is better nor the breid?

" O what is whiter nor the milk?
Or what is safter nor the silk?

" Or what is sharper nor a thorn?
Or what is louder nor a horn?

"Or what is greener nor the grass?
  Or what is waur nor a woman was?"

"O heaven is higher nor the tree,
  And hell is deeper nor the sea.

"O sin is heavier nor the lead,
  The blessing's better nor the breid.

"The snaw is whiter nor the milk,
  And the down is safter nor the silk.

"Hunger is sharper nor a thorn,
  And shame is louder nor a horn.

"The pies are greener nor the grass,
  And Clootie's waur nor a woman was."

As sune as she the fiend did name,
    Jennifer gentle an' rosemaree,
He flew awa in a blazing flame,
    As the dew flies ower the mulberry tree.

BALLADS OF TRADITION.

BALLADS OF TRADITION.

SIR PATRICK SPENS.

The King sits in Dunfermline toun,
    Drinking the blude-red wine ;
"O whaur shall I get a skeely skipper,
    To sail this gude ship of mine ? "

Then up an' spake an eldern knight,
    Sat at the King's right knee ;
"Sir Patrick Spens is the best sailor
    That ever sailed the sea."

The King has written a braid letter,
    And seal'd it wi' his hand,
And sent it to Sir Patrick Spens
    Was walking on the sand.

"To Noroway, to Noroway,
    To Noroway o'er the faem ;
The King's daughter to Noroway,
    It's thou maun tak' her hame."

The first line that Sir Patrick read,
    A loud laugh laughed he,
The neist line that Sir Patrick read,
    The tear blinded his e'e.

"O wha is this hae dune this deed,
   And tauld the King o' me,
To send us out at this time o' the year
   To sail upon the sea ?

"Be it wind or weet, be it hail or sleet,
   Our ship maun sail the faem,
The King's daughter to Noroway,
   'Tis we maun tak' her hame."

They hoisted their sails on Monday morn,
   Wi' a' the speed they may ;
And they hae landed in Noroway
   Upon the Wodensday.

They hadna been a week, a week,
   In Noroway but twae,
When that the lords o' Noroway·
   Began aloud to say —

"Ye Scotsmen spend a' our King's gowd,
   And a' our Queenis fee."
"Ye lie, ye lie, ye liars loud,
   Sae loud's I hear ye lie !

"For I brouct as mickle white monie,
   As gane my men and me,
And a half-fou o' the gude red gold,
   Out owre the sea wi' me.

"Mak' ready, mak' ready, my merry men a',
    Our gude ship sails the morn."
"Now ever alack, my master dear,
    I fear a deadly storm.

"I saw the new moon late yestreen,
    Wi' the auld moon in her arm;
And I fear, I fear, my master dear,
    That we sall come to harm!"

They hadna sail'd a league, a league,
    A league but barely three,
When the lift grew dark, and the wind blew loud,
    And gurly grew the sea.

The ropes they brak, and the top-masts lap,
    It was sic a deadly storm;
And the waves cam' o'er the broken ship,
    Till a' her sides were torn.

"O whaur will I get a gude sailor
    Will tak' the helm in hand,
Until I win to the tall top-mast,
    And see if I spy the land?"

"It's here am I, a sailor gude,
    Will tak' the helm in hand,
Till ye win to the tall top-mast,
    But I fear ye'll ne'er spy land."

He hadna gane a step, a step,
   A step but barely ane,
When a bolt flew out of the gude ship's side,
   And the saut sea it cam' in.

"Gae, fetch a web of the silken claith,
   Anither o' the twine,
And wap them into the gude ship's side,
   And let na the sea come in."

They fetched a web o' the silken claith,
   Anither o' the twine,
And they wapp'd them into that gude ship's side,
   But aye the sea cam' in.

O laith, laith, were our gude Scots lords
   To weet their cock-heeled shoon,
But lang ere a' the play was o'er
   They wat their hats abune.

O laith, laith were our gude Scots lords
   To weet their milk-white hands,
But lang ere a' the play was played
   They wat their gouden bands.

O lang, lang may the ladies sit,
   Wi' their fans into their hand,
Or ever they see Sir Patrick Spens
   Come sailing to the land.

O lang, lang may the maidens sit,
  Wi' their gowd kaims in their hair,
A' waiting for their ain dear loves,
  For them they'll see nae mair.

Half owre, half owre to Aberdour,
  It's fifty fathom deep,
And there lies gude Sir Patrick Spens,
  Wi' the Scots lords at his feet.

THE BATTLE OF OTTERBURNE.

IT fell about the Lammas tide,
  When muirmen win their hay,
That the doughty Earl of Douglas rade
  Into England to fetch a prey.

And he has ta'en the Lindsays light,
  With them the Gordons gay;
But the Jardines wad not with him ride,
  And they rue it to this day.

Then they hae harried the dales o' Tyne,
  And half o' Bambrough-shire,
And the Otter-dale they burned it haill,
  And set it a' on fire.

Then he cam' up to New Castel,
　　And rade it round about:
" O who is the lord of this castel,
　　Or who is the lady o't ? "

But up and spake Lord Percy then,
　　And O but he spake hie:
" It's I am the lord of this castel,
　　My wife is the lady gay."

" If thou'rt the lord of this castel,
　　Sae weel it pleases me !
For ere I cross the Border fell,
　　The tane of us shall dee." —

He took a lang spear in his hand,
　　Shod with the metal free;
And forth to meet the Douglas then,
　　He rade richt furiouslie.

But O how pale his lady looked
　　Frae aff the castle wa',
As doun before the Scottish spear
　　She saw proud Percy fa' !

" Had we twa been upon the green,
　　And never an eye to see,
I wad hae had you, flesh and fell,
　　But your sword shall gae wi' me."

" Now gae up to the Otterburne,
 And bide there dayis three,
And gin I come not ere they end,
 A fause knight ca' ye me!"

" The Otterburne is a bonnie burn,
 'Tis pleasant there to be;
But there is nought at Otterburne
 To feed my men and me.

" The deer rins wild on hill and dale,
 The birds fly wild frae tree to tree;
But there is neither bread nor kale,
 To fend my men and me.

" Yet I will stay at the Otterburne,
 Where you shall welcome be;
And, if ye come not at three dayis end,
 A fause lord I'll ca' thee."

" Thither will I come," Earl Percy said,
 By the might of our Ladye!"
" There will I bide thee," said the Douglas,
 " My troth I plight to thee!"

They lichted high on Otterburne,
 Upon the bent sae broun;
They lichted high on Otterburne,
 And pitched their pallions doun.

And he that had a bonnie boy,
   He sent his horse to grass;
And he that had not a bonnie boy,
   His ain servant he was.

Then up and spake a little boy,
   Was near of Douglas' kin —
" Methinks I see an English host
   Come branking us upon!

" Nine wargangs beiring braid and wide,
   Seven banners beiring high;
It wad do any living gude,
   To see their colours fly!"

" If this be true, my little boy,
   That thou tells unto me,
The brawest bower o' the Otterburne
   Sall be thy morning fee.

" But I hae dreamed a dreary dream,
   Ayont the Isle o' Skye, —
I saw a deid man win a fight,
   And I think that man was I."

He belted on his gude braid-sword,
   And to the field he ran;
But he forgot the hewmont strong,
   That should have kept his brain.

When Percy wi' the Douglas met,
    I wot he was fu' fain:
They swakkit swords, and they twa swat,
    Till the blude ran down like rain.

But Percy wi' his gude braid-sword,
    That could sae sharply wound,
Has wounded Douglas on the brow,
    That he fell to the ground.

And then he called his little foot-page,
    And said — " Run speedilie,
And fetch my ae dear sister's son,
    Sir Hugh Montgomerie,

" My nephew gude ! " the Douglas said,
    " What recks the death of ane ?
Last night I dreamed a dreary dream,
    And ken the day's thy ain !

" My wound is deep ; I fain wad sleep !
    Tak' thou the vanguard o' the three,
And bury me by the bracken bush,
    That grows on yonder lily lea.

" O bury me by the bracken bush,
    Beneath the blumin' brier ;
Let never living mortal ken
    That a kindly Scot lies here ! "

He lifted up that noble lord,
　Wi' the saut tear in his e'e;
And he hid him by the bracken bush,
　That his merry men might not see.

The moon was clear, the day drew near,
　The spears in flinders flew;
And many a gallant Englishman
　Ere day the Scotsmen slew.

The Gordons gay, in English blude
　They wat their hose and shoon;
The Lindsays flew like fire about,
　Till a' the fray was dune.

The Percy and Montgomery met,
　That either of other was fain;
They swakkit swords, and sair they swat,
　And the blude ran down between.

" Now yield thee, yield thee, Percy!" he said,
　Or else I will lay thee low!"
" To whom maun I yield," Earl Percy said,
　" Since I see that it maun be so?"

" Thou shalt not yield to lord or loun,
　Nor yet shalt thou yield to me;
But yield thee to the bracken-bush
　That grows on yonder lily lea!"

This deed was done at the Otterburne
  About the breaking o' the day;
Earl Douglas was buried at the bracken bush,
  And the Percy led captive away.

THE HUNTING OF THE CHEVIOT.

THE FIRST FIT.

THE Persè owt off Northombarlande,
  And a vowe to God mayd he,
That he wold hunte in the mountayns
  Off Chyviat within days thre,
In the mauger of doughtè Dogles,
  And all that ever with him be.

The fattiste hartes in all Cheviat
  He sayd he wold kill, and cary them away:
"Be my feth," sayd the dougheti Doglas agayn,
  "I wyll let that hontyng, yf that I may."

Then the Persè owt of Banborowe cam,
  With him a myghtye meany;
With fifteen hondrith archares bold;
  The wear chosen owt of shyars thre.

This begane on a monday at morn,
  In Cheviat the hillys so he;
The chyld may rue that ys un-born,
  It was the mor pittè.

The dryvars thorowe the woodès went,
   For to reas the dear;
Bomen byckarte uppone the bent
   With ther browd aras cleare.

Then the wyld thorowe the woodès went,
   On every sydè shear;
Grea-hondes thorowe the grevis glent,
   For to kyll thear dear.

The begane in Chyviat the hyls above,
   Yerly on a monnynday;
Be that it drewe to the oware off none,
   A hondrith fat hartes ded ther lay.

The blewe a mort uppone the bent,
   The semblyd on sydis shear;
To the quyrry then the Persè went
   To se the bryttlynge off the deare.

He sayd, "It was the Duglas promys
   This day to meet me hear;
But I wyste he wold faylle, verament:"
   A gret oth the Persè swear.

At the laste a squyar of Northombelonde
   Lokyde at his hand full ny;
He was war ath the doughetie Doglas comynge,
   With him a myghtè meany;

Both with spear, byll, and brande;
   Yt was a myghti sight to se;
Hardyar men both off hart nar hande
   Wear not in Christiantè.

The wear twenty hondrith spear-men good,
   Withowtè any fayle;
The wear borne along be the watter a Twyde,
   Yth bowndes of Tividale.

"Leave off the brytlyng of the dear," he sayde,
   "And to your bowys lock ye tayk good heed;
For never sithe ye wear on your mothars borne
   Had ye never so mickle need."

The dougheti Dogglas on a stede
   He rode aft his men beforne;
His armor glytteryde as dyd a glede;
   A bolder barne was never born.

"Tell me what men ye ar," he says,
   "Or whos men that ye be:
Who gave youe leave to hunte in this Chyviat chays,
   In the spyt of me?"

The first mane that ever him an answear mayd,
   Yt was the good lord Persè:
We wyll not tell the what men we ar," he says,
   "Nor whos men that we be;
But we wyll hount hear in this chays,
   In the spyt of thyne and of the.

" The fattiste hartes in all Chyviat
    We have kyld, and cast to carry them a-way : "
"Be my troth," sayd the doughtè Dogglas agayn,
    " Ther-for the ton of us shall de this day."

    Then sayd the doughtè Doglas
        Unto the lord Persè :
" To kyll all thes giltles men,
    Alas, it were great pittè !

" But, Persè, thowe art a lord of lande,
    I am a yerle callyd within my contrè ;
Let all our men uppone a parti stande,
    And do the battell off the and of me."

" Nowe Cristes cors on his crowne," sayd the lord Persè,
    " Whosoever ther-to says nay ;
Be my troth, doughtè Doglas," he says,
    " Thow shalt never se that day.

" Nethar in Ynglonde, Skottlonde, nar France,
    Nor for no man of a woman born,
But, and fortune be my chance,
    I dar met him, on man for on."

    Then bespayke a squyar off Northombarlonde,
    Richard Wytharynton was him nam ;
" It shall never be told in Sothe-Ynglonde," he says,
    " To kyng Herry the fourth for sham.

" I wat youe byn great lordes twaw,
 I am a poor squyar of lande ;
I wyll never se my captayne fyght on a fylde,
 And stande myselffe, and looke on,
But whyll I may my weppone welde,
 I wyll not ffayll both hart and hande."

That day, that day, that dredfull day !
 The first fit here I fynde ;
And youe wyll here any mor a' the hountyng a'
  the Chyviat,
 Yet ys ther mor behynd.

THE SECOND FIT.

The Yngglyshe men hade ther bowys yebent,
 Ther hartes were good yenoughe ;
The first off arros that the shote off,
 Seven skore spear-men the sloughe.

Yet byddys the yerle Doglas uppon the bent,
 A captayne good yenoughe,
And that was sene verament,
 For he wrought hom both woo and wouche.

The Dogglas pertyd his ost in thre,
 Lyk a cheffe cheften off pryde,
With suar speares off myghttè tre,
 The cum in on every syde :

Thrughe our Yngglishe archery
  Gave many a wounde full wyde;
Many a doughete the garde to dy,
  Which ganyde them no pryde.

The Yngglyshe men let thear bowys be,
  And pulde owt brandes that wer bright;
It was a hevy syght to se
  Bryght swordes on basnites lyght.

Throrowe ryche male and myneyeple,
  Many sterne the stroke downe streght;
Many a freyke, that was full fre,
  Ther undar foot dyd lyght.

At last the Duglas and the Persè met,
  Lyk to captayns of myght and of mayne;
The swapte togethar tyll the both swat,
  With swordes that wear of fyn myllàn.

Thes worthè freckys for to fyght,
  Ther-to the wear full fayne,
Tyll the bloode owte off thear basnetes sprente,
  As ever dyd heal or rayne.

" Holde the, Persè," sayd the Doglas,
  " And i' feth I shall the brynge
Wher thowe shalte have a yerls wagis
  Of Jamy our Scottish kynge.

"Thoue shalte have thy ranson fre,
   I hight the hear this thinge,
For the manfullyste man yet art thowe,
   That ever I conqueryd in filde fightyng."

"Nay," sayd the lord Persè,
   "I tolde it the beforne,
That I wolde never yeldyde be
   To no man of woman born."

With that ther cam an arrowe hastely
   Forthe off a myghttè wane ;
Hit hathe strekene the yerle Duglas
   In at the brest bane.

Thoroue lyvar and longs bathe
   The sharp arrowe ys gane,
That never after in all his lyffe-days,
   He spayke mo wordes but ane :
That was, "Fyghte ye, my merry men, whyllys ye may,
   For my lyff-days ben gan."

The Persè leanyde on his brande,
   And sawe the Duglas de ;
He tooke the dede man be the hande,
   And sayd, "Wo ys me for the !

"To have savyde thy lyffe I wolde have pertyde with
   My landes for years thre,
For a better man, of hart nare of hande,
   Was not in all the north contrè."

Off all that se a Skottishe knyght,
  Was callyd Sir Hewe the Mongonbyrry;
He sawe the Duglas to the deth was dyght,
  He spendyd a spear, a trusti tre : —

He rod uppon a corsiare
  Throughe a hondrith archery :
He never styntyde, nar never blane,
  Tyll he cam to the good lord Persè.

He set uppone the lord Persè
  A dynte that was full soare ;
With a suar spear of a myghttè tre
  Clean thorow the body he the Persè bore,

A' the tother syde that a man myght se
  A large cloth yard and mare :
Towe bettar captayns wear nat in Christiantè,
  Then that day slain wear ther.

An archar off Northomberlonde
  Say slean was the lord Persè ;
He bar a bende-bowe in his hande,
  Was made off trusti tre.

An arow, that a cloth yarde was lang,
  To th' hard stele halyde he ;
A dynt that was both sad and soar,
  He sat on Sir Hewe the Mongonbyrry.

The dynt yt was both sad and sar,
   That he on Mongonberry sete ;
The swane-fethars, that his arrowe bar,
   With his hart-blood the wear wete.

Ther was never a freake wone foot wolde fle,
   But still in stour dyd stand,
Heawyng on yche othar, whyll the myght dre,
   With many a balful brande.

This battell begane in Chyviat
   An owar befor the none,
And when even-song bell was rang,
   The battell was nat half done.

The tooke on ethar hand
   Be the lyght off the mone ;
Many hade no strenght for to stande,
   In Chyviat the hillys aboun.

Of fifteen hondrith archars of Yonglonde
   Went away but fifti and thre ;
Of twenty hondrith spear-men of Skotlonde,
   But even five and fifti :

But all wear slayne Cheviat within ;
   The hade no strengthe to stand on hie ;
The chylde may rue that ys unborne,
   It was the mor pittè.

Thear was slayne with the lord Persè
    Sir John of Agerstone,
Sir Rogar the hinde Hartly,
    Sir Wyllyam the bolde Hearone.

Sir Jorg the worthè Lovele,
    A knyght of great renowen,
Sir Raff the ryche Rugbè,
    With dyntes wear beaten dowene.

For Wetharryngton my harte was wo,
    That ever he slayne shulde be ;
For when both his leggis wear hewyne in to,
    Yet he knyled and fought on hys kne.

Ther was slayne with the dougheti Douglas,
    Sir Hewe the Mongonbyrry,
Sir Davye Lwdale, that worthè was,
    His sistars son was he :

His Charls a Murrè in that place,
    That never a foot wolde fle ;
Sir Hewe Maxwell, a lorde he was,
    With the Duglas dyd he dey.

So on the morrowe the mayde them byears
    Off birch and hasell so gray ;
Many wedous with wepyng tears
    Cam to fach ther makys away.

Tivydale may carpe off care,
   Northombarlond may mayk grat mon,
For towe such captayns as slayne wear thear,
   On the march perti shall never be non.

Word ys commen to Eddenburrowe,
   To Jamy the Skottishe kyng,
That dougheti Duglas, lyff-tenant of the Merches,
   He lay slean Chyviot with-in.

His handdes dyd he weal and wryng,
   He sayd, "Alas, and woe ys me!
"Such an othar captayn Skotland within,"
   He sayd, "y-feth shall never be."

Worde ys commyn to lovly Londone,
   Till the fourth Harry our kyng,
That lord Persè, lyffe-tennante of the Merchis,
   He lay slayne Chyviat within.

"God have merci on his soll," sayd kyng Harry,
   "Good lord, yf thy will it be!
I have a hondrith captayns in Ynglonde," he sayd,
   "As good as ever was hee:
But Persè, and I brook my lyffe,
   Thy deth well quyte shall be."

As our noble kyng mayd his a-vowe,
   Lyke a noble prince of renowen,
For the deth of the lord Persè
   He dyde the battell of Hombyll-down:

Wher syx and thritté Skottishe knyghtes
  On a day wear beaten down ;
Glendale glytteryde on ther armor bryght,
  Over castill, towar, and town.

This was the Hontynge off the Cheviat ;
  That tear begane this spurn :
Old men that knowen the grownde well yenoughe,
  Call it the Battell of Otterburn.

At Otterburn began this spurne
  Uppon a monnynday :
Ther was the dougghtè Doglas slean,
  The Persè never went away.

Ther was never a tym on the March partes
  Sen the Doglas and the Persè met,
But yt was marvele, and the redde blude ronne not,
  As the reane doys in the stret.

Jhesue Christ our balys bete,
  And to the blys us brynge !
Thus was the Hountynge of the Chevyat :
  God send us all good endyng.

EDOM O' GORDON.

It fell about the Martinmas,
 When the wind blew shrill and cauld,
Said Edom o' Gordon to his men,
 "We maun draw to a hauld.

"And whatna hauld sall we draw to,
 My merry men and me?
We will gae to the house o' the Rodes,
 To see that fair ladie."

The ladie stude on her castle wa',
 Beheld baith dale and down,
There she was ware of a host of men
 Were riding towards the town.

"O see ye not, my merry men a',
 O see ye not what I see?
Methinks I see a host of men —
 I marvel what they be."

She ween'd it had been her ain dear lord
 As he cam' riding hame;
It was the traitor, Edom o' Gordon,
 Wha recked nor sin nor shame.

She had nae suner buskit hersell,
   Nor putten on her goun,
Till Edom o' Gordon and his men
   Were round about the toun.

They had nae suner supper set,
   Nor suner said the grace,
Till Edom o' Gordon and his men
   Were light about the place.

The ladie ran to her tower head,
   As fast as she could hie,
To see if, by her fair speeches,
   She could with him agree.

"Come doun to me, ye ladye gay,
   Come doun, come doun to me;
This nicht sall ye lie within my arms,
   The morn my bride sall be."

"I winna come doun, ye fause Gordon,
   I winna come doun to thee;
I winna forsake my ain dear lord,
   That is sae far frae me."

"Gie owre your house, ye ladie fair,
   Gie owre your house to me;
Or I sall burn yoursell therein,
   But and your babies three."

"I winna gie owre, ye false Gordon,
    To nae sic traitor as thee;
And if ye burn my ain dear babes,
    My lord sall mak' ye dree!

"But reach my pistol, Glaud, my man,
    And charge ye weel my gun;
For, but an I pierce that bludy butcher,
    We a' sall be undone."

She stude upon the castle wa',
    And let twa bullets flee;
She miss'd that bludy butcher's heart,
    And only razed his knee.

"Set fire to the house!" quo' the false Gordon,
    All wude wi' dule and ire;
"False ladie! ye sall rue that shot,
    As ye burn in the fire."

"Wae worth, wae worth ye, Jock, my man!
    I paid ye weel your fee;
Why pu' ye out the grund-wa-stane,
    Lets in the reek to me?

"And e'en wae worth ye, Jock, my man!
    I paid ye weel your hire;
Why pu' ye out my grund-wa-stane,
    To me lets in the fire?"

"Ye paid me weel my hire, lady,
 Ye paid me weel my fee;
But now I'm Edom o' Gordon's man,
 Maun either do or die."

O then bespake her youngest son,
 Sat on the nourice' knee;
Says, "Mither dear, gie owre this house,
 For the reek it smothers me."

"I wad gie a' my gowd, my bairn,
 Sae wad I a' my fee,
For ae blast o' the westlin' wind,
 To blaw the reek frae thee!"

O then bespake her daughter dear—
 She was baith jimp and sma'—
"O row me in a pair o' sheets,
 And tow me owre the wa'."

They rowed her in a pair o' sheets,
 And towed her owre the wa';
But on the point o' Gordon's spear
 She gat a deadly fa'.

O bonnie, bonnie was her mouth,
 And cherry were her cheeks;
And clear, clear was her yellow hair,
 Whereon the red blude dreeps.

Then wi' his spear he turned her owre,
   O gin her face was wan!
He said, "You are the first that e'er
   I wish'd alive again."

He turned her owre and owre again,
   O gin her skin was white!
"I might hae spared that bonnie face,
   To hae been some man's delight.

"Busk and boun, my merry men a',
   For ill dooms I do guess;
I canna look on that bonnie face,
   As it lies on the grass!"

"Wha looks to freits, my master deir,
   It's freits will follow them;
Let it ne'er be said that Edom o' Gordon
   Was dauntit by a dame."

But when the lady saw the fire
   Come flaming owre her head,
She wept, and kiss'd her children twain,
   Says, "Bairns, we been but dead."

The Gordon then his bugle blew,
   And said, "Awa', awa';
The house o' the Rodes is a' in a flame,
   I hold it time to ga'."

O then bespied her ain dear lord,
   As he came owre the lee;
He saw his castle all in a lowe,
   Sae far as he could see.

"Put on, put on, my wichty men,
   As fast as ye can dri'e;
For he that is hindmost of the thrang,
   Shall ne'er get gude o' me!"

Then some they rade, and some they ran,
   Fu' fast out-owre the bent;
But ere the foremost could win up,
   Baith lady and babes were brent.

He wrang his hands, he rent his hair,
   And wept in teenfu' mood;
"Ah, traitors! for this cruel deed,
   Ye shall weep tears of blude."

And after the Gordon he has gane,
   Sae fast as he might dri'e,
And soon i' the Gordon's foul heart's blude,
   He's wroken his fair ladie.

KINMONT WILLIE.

O HAVE ye na heard o' the fause Sakelde ?
　　O have ye na heard o' the keen Lord Scroope ?
How they hae ta'en bauld Kinmont Willie,
　　On Haribee to hang him up ?

Had Willie had but twenty men,
　　But twenty men as stout as he,
Fause Sakelde had never the Kinmont ta'en,
　　Wi' eight score in his companie.

They band his legs beneath the steed,
　　They tied his hands behind his back ;
They guarded him, fivesome on each side,
　　And they brought him ower the Liddel-rack.

They led him thro' the Liddel-rack,
　　And also thro' the Carlisle sands ;
They brought him on to Carlisle castle,
　　To be at my Lord Scroope's commands.

"My hands are tied, but my tongue is free,
　　And wha will dare this deed avow ?
Or answer by the Border law ?
　　Or answer to the bauld Buccleuch ? "

"Now haud thy tongue, thou rank reiver!
  There's never a Scot shall set thee free:
 Before ye cross my castle yate
  I trow ye shall take farewell o' me."

"Fear ye na that, my lord," quo' Willie:
  "By the faith o' my body, Lord Scroope," he said
"I never yet lodged in a hostelrie,
  But I paid my lawing before I gaed."

Now word is gane to the bauld keeper,
  In Branksome Ha', where that he lay,
That Lord Scroope has ta'en the Kinmont Willie,
  Between the hours of night and day.

He has ta'en the table wi' his hand,
  He garr'd the red wine spring on hie,
"Now a curse upon my head," he said,
  "But avengèd of Lord Scroope I'll be!

"O is my basnet a widow's curch?
  Or my lance a wand of the willow-tree?
 Or my arm a lady's lily hand,
  That an English lord should lightly me?

"And have they ta'en him, Kinmont Willie,
  Against the truce of Border tide,
And forgotten that the bauld Buccleuch
  Is Keeper here on the Scottish side?

"And have they e'en ta'en him, Kinmont Willie,
    Withouten either dread or fear,
And forgotten that the bauld Buccleuch
    Can back a steed, or shake a spear?

"O were there war between the lands,
    As well I wot that there is nane,
I would slight Carlisle castle high,
    Though it were builded of marble stane.

"I would set that castle in a low,
    And sloken it with English blood!
There's never a man in Cumberland
    Should ken where Carlisle castle stood.

"But since nae war's between the lands,
    And there is peace, and peace should be,
I'll neither harm English lad or lass,
    And yet the Kinmont freed shall be!"

He has called him forty Marchmen bauld,
    I trow they were of his ain name,
Except Sir Gilbert Elliot, called
    The Laird of Stobs, I mean the same.

He has called him forty Marchmen bauld,
    Were kinsmen to the bauld Buccleuch;
With spur on heel, and splent on spauld,
    And gluves of green, and feathers blue.

There were five and five before them a',
    Wi' hunting horns and bugles bright :
And five and five cam' wi' Buccleuch,
    Like warden's men, arrayed for fight.

And five and five, like masons gang,
    That carried the ladders lang and hie ;
And five and five like broken men ;
    And so they reached the Woodhouselee.

And as we crossed the 'Bateable Land,
    When to the English side we held,
The first o' men that we met wi',
    Wha sould it be but fause Sakelde ?

" Where be ye gaun, ye hunters keen ? "
    Quo' fause Sakelde ; "come tell to me ! "
" We go to hunt an English stag,
    Has trespassed on the Scots countrie."

" Where be ye gaun, ye marshal men ? "
    Quo' fause Sakelde ; "come tell me true ! "
" We go to catch a rank reiver,
    Has broken faith wi' the bauld Buccleuch."

" Where are ye gaun, ye mason lads,
    Wi' a' your ladders lang and hie ? "
" We gang to herry a corbie's nest,
    That wons not far frae Woodhouselee."

" Where be ye gaun, ye broken men ? "
 Quo' fause Sakelde ; "come tell to me !"
Now Dickie of Dryhope led that band,
 And the nevir a word of lear had he.

" Why trespass ye on the English side ?
 Row-footed outlaws, stand !" quo' he ;
The nevir a word had Dickie to say,
 Sae he thrust the lance through his fause bodie.

Then on we held for Carlisle toun,
 And at Staneshaw-bank the Eden we crossed,
The water was great and meikle of spait,
 But the never a horse nor man we lost.

And when we reached the Staneshaw-bank,
 The wind was rising loud and hie ;
And there the Laird garr'd leave our steeds,
 For fear that they should stamp and neigh.

And when we left the Staneshaw-bank,
 The wind began full loud to blaw ;
But 'twas wind and weet, and fire and sleet,
 When we cam' beneath the castle wa'.

We crept on knees, and held our breath,
 Till we placed the ladders agin the wa' ;
And sae ready was Buccleuch himsell
 To mount the first before us a'.

He has ta'en the watchman by the throat,
   He flung him down upon the lead :
"Had there not been peace between our lands,
   Upon the other side thou hadst gaed !

"Now sound out, trumpets !" quo' Buccleuch ;
   "Let's waken Lord Scroope right merrilie !"
Then loud the warden's trumpet blew —
   O wha dare meddle wi' me?

Then speedilie to wark we gaed,
   And raised the slogan ane and a',
And cut a hole through a sheet of lead,
   And so we wan to the castle ha'.

They thought King James and a' his men
   Had won the house wi' bow and spear ;
It was but twenty Scots and ten,
   That put a thousand in sic a stear !

Wi' coulters, and wi' forehammers,
   We garr'd the bars bang merrilie,
Until we cam' to the inner prison,
   Where Willie o' Kinmont he did lie.

And when we cam' to the lower prison,
   Where Willie o' Kinmont he did lie, —
"O sleep ye, wake ye, Kinmont Willie,
   Upon the morn that thou's to die ?"

"O I sleep saft, and I wake aft;
    It's lang since sleeping was fley'd frae me;
Gie my service back to my wife and bairns,
    And a' gude fellows that spier for me."

Then Red Rowan has hente him up,
    The starkest man in Teviotdale, —
"Abide, abide now, Red Rowan,
    Till of my Lord Scroope I tak' farewell.

"Farewell, farewell, my gude Lord Scroope!
    My gude Lord Scroope, farewell!" he cried:
"I'll pay you for my lodging maill,
    When first we meet on the Border side."

Then shoulder high, with shout and cry,
    We bore him doun the ladder lang;
At every stride Red Rowan made,
    I wot the Kinmont's airns played clang

"O mony a time," quo' Kinmont Willie,
    "I have ridden horse baith wild and wood;
But a rougher beast than Red Rowan
    I ween my legs have ne'er bestrode.

"And mony a time," quo' Kinmont Willie,
    I've pricked a horse out oure the furs;
But since the day I backed a steed,
    I never wore sic cumbrous spurs."

We scarce had won the Staneshaw-bank,
　　When a' the Carlisle bells were rung,
And a thousand men on horse and foot
　　Cam' wi' the·keen Lord Scroope along.

Buccleuch has turned to Eden Water,
　　Even where it flowed frae bank to brim,
And he has plunged in wi' a' his band,
　　And safely swam them through the stream.

He turned him on the other side,
　　And at Lord Scroope his glove flung he :
"If ye like na my visit in merry England,
　　In fair Scotland come visit me !"

All sore astonished stood Lord Scroope,
　　He stood as still as rock of stane ;
He scarcely dared to trew his eyes,
　　When through the water they had gane.

"He is either himsell a devil frae hell,
　　Or else his mither a witch maun be ;
I wadna hae ridden that wan water
　　For a' the gowd in Christentie."

KING JOHN AND THE ABBOT OF CANTERBURY.

AN ancient story Ile tell you anon
Of a notable prince, that was called King John;
He ruled over England with maine and with might,
For he did great wrong, and mainteined little right.

And Ile tell you a story, a story so merrye,
Concerning the Abbot of Canterburye;
How for his housekeeping and high renowne,
They rode poste for him to fair London towne.

A hundred men, for the king did hear say,
The abbot kept in his house every day;
And fifty golde chaynes, without any doubt,
In velvet coates waited the abbot about.

" How now, father abbot ? I heare it of thee,
Thou keepest a farre better house than mee;
And for thy housekeeping and high renowne,
I feare thou work'st treason against my crown."

" My liege," quo' the abbot, "I would it were knowne,
I never spend nothing but what is my owne;
And I trust your grace will doe me no deere,
For spending of my owne true-gotten geere."

" Yes, yes, father abbot, thy faulte it is highe,
  And now for the same thou needest must dye ;
  And except thou canst answer me questions three,
  Thy head shall be smitten from thy bodie.

" And first," quo' the king, " when I'm in this stead,
  With my crown of golde so faire on my head,
  Among all my liegemen so noble of birthe,
  Thou must tell to one penny what I am worthe.

" Secondlye, tell me, without any doubt,
  How soon I may ride the whole world about ;
  And at the third question thou must not shrink,
  But tell me here truly, what I do think ? "

" O, these are deep questions for my shallow witt,
  Nor I cannot answer your grace as yet :
  But if you will give me but three weekes space,
  I'll do my endeavor to answer your grace."

" Now three weekes space to thee will I give,
  And that is the longest thou hast to live ;
  For unless thou answer my questions three,
  Thy life and thy lands are forfeit to mee."

  Away rode the abbot all sad at this word ;
  And he rode to Cambridge and Oxenford ;
  But never a doctor there was so wise,
  That could with his learning an answer devise.

Then home rode the Abbot of comfort so cold,
And he mett his shepheard a going to fold:
" How now, my lord abbot, you are welcome home;
What newes do you bring us from good king John?"

" Sad newes, sad newes, shepheard, I must give;
That I have but three days more to live;
For if I do not answer him questions three,
My head will be smitten from my bodie.

" The first is to tell him, there in that stead,
With his crowne of golde so fair on his head,
Among all his liege men so noble of birth,
To within one penny of what he is worth.

" The seconde, to tell him, without any doubt,
How soone he may ride this whole world about;
And at the third question I must not shrinke,
But tell him there trulye what he does thinke."

" Now cheare up, sire abbot, did you never hear yet,
That a fool he may learne a wise man witt?
Lend me horse, and serving men, and your apparel,
And Ile ride to London to answere your quarrel.

" Nay frowne not, if it hath bin told unto mee,
I am like your lordship, as ever may bee;
And if you will but lend me your gowne,
There is none shall knowe us at fair London towne.

" Now horses and serving men thou shalt have,
   With sumptuous array most gallant and brave;
   With crosier, and miter, and rochet, and cope,
   Fit to appear 'fore our fader the pope."

" Now welcome, sire abbot," the king he did say,
" 'Tis well thou'rt come back to keepe thy day;
   For and if thou canst answer my questions three,
   Thy life and thy living both saved shall bee.

" And first, when thou seest me here in this stead,
   With my crown of golde so faire on my head,
   Among all my liege men so noble of birthe,
   Tell me to one penny what I am worth."

" For thirty pence our Savior was sold
   Amonge the false Jewes, as I have bin told;
   And twenty-nine is the worth of thee,
   For I thinke, thou art one penny worser than hee."

The king he laughed, and swore by St. Bittel,
" I did not think I had been worth so littel!
   — Now secondly tell me, without any doubt,
   How soone I may ride this whole world about."

" You must rise with the sun, and ride with the same
   Until the next morning he riseth againe;
   And then your grace need not make any doubt,
   But in twenty-four hours you'll ride it about."

The king he laughed, and swore "by St. Jone,
I did not think it could be gone so soone!
— Now from the third question thou must not shrinke,
But tell me here truly what I do thinke."

" Yea, that shall I do, and make your grace merry:
You thinke I'm the abbot of Canterbùry;
But I'm his poor shepheard, as plain you may see,
That am come to beg pardon for him and for mee."

The king he laughed, and swore "by the masse,
Ile make thee lord abbot this day in his place!"
" Now naye, my liege, be not in such speede;
For alacke I can neither write ne reade."

" Four nobles a week, then, I will give thee,
For this merry jest thou hast shown unto mee;
And tell the old abbot, when thou comest home,
Thou hast brought him a pardon from good king John."

ROBIN HOOD RESCUING THE WIDOW'S THREE SONS.

THERE are twelve months in all the year,
    As I hear many say,
But the merriest month in all the year
    Is the merry month of May.

Now Robin Hood is to Nottingham gone,
    With a link a down and a day,
And there he met a silly old woman,
    Was weeping on the way.

"What news? what news, thou silly old woman?
　　What news hast thou for me?"
　Said she, "There's my three sons in Nottingham tow
　　To-day condemned to die."

"O, have they parishes burnt?" he said,
　　"Or have they ministers slain?
　Or have they robbed any virgin?
　　Or other men's wives have ta'en?"

"They have no parishes burnt, good sir,
　　Nor yet have ministers slain,
　Nor have they robbed any virgin,
　　Nor other men's wives have ta'en."

"O, what have they done?" said Robin Hood,
　　"I pray thee tell to me."
"It's for slaying of the king's fallow-deer,
　　Bearing their long bows with thee."

"Dost thou not mind, old woman," he said,
　　"How thou madest me sup and dine?
　By the truth of my body," quoth bold Robin Hood,
　　"You could not tell it in better time."

　Now Robin Hood is to Nottingham gone,
　　With a link a down and a day,
　And there he met with a silly old palmer,
　　Was walking along the highway.

"What news ? what news, thou silly old man ?
  What news, I do thee pray ? "
Said he, "Three squires in Nottingham town
  Are condemned to die this day."

"Come change thy apparel with me, old man,
  Come change thy apparel for mine ;
Here is forty shillings in good silvèr,
  Go drink it in beer or wine."

"O, thine apparel is good," he said,
  "And mine is ragged and torn ;
Wherever you go, wherever you ride,
  Laugh ne'er an old man to scorn."

"Come change thy apparel with me, old churl,
  Come change thy apparel with mine ;
Here are twenty pieces of good broad gold,
  Go feast thy brethren with wine."

Then he put on the old man's hat,
  It stood full high on the crown :
"The first bold bargain that I come at,
  It shall make thee come down."

Then he put on the old man's cloak,
  Was patched black, blew, and red ;
He thought it no shame all the day long,
  To wear the bags of bread.

Then he put on the old man's breeks,
    Was patched from leg to side :
"By the truth of my body," bold Robin can say,
    "This man loved little pride."

Then he put on the old man's hose,
    Were patched from knee to wrist :
"By the truth of my body," said bold Robin Hood,
    "I'd laugh if I had any list."

Then he put on the old man's shoes,
    Were patched both beneath and aboon ;
Then Robin Hood swore a solemn oath,
    "It's good habit that makes a man."

Now Robin Hood is to Nottingham gone,
    With a link a down and a down,
And there he met with the proud sheriff,
    Was walking along the town.

"O Christ you save, O sheriff !" he said ;
    "O Christ you save and see !
And what will you give to a silly old man
    To-day will your hangman be ? "

"Some suits, some suits," the sheriff he said,
    "Some suits I'll give to thee ;
Some suits, some suits, and pence thirteen,
    To-day's a hangman's fee."

Then Robin he turns him round about,
    And jumps from stock to stone :
"By the truth of my body," the sheriff he said,
    "That's well jumpt, thou nimble old man."

"I was ne'er a hangman in all my life,
    Nor yet intends to trade ;
But curst be he," said bold Robin,
    "That first a hangman was made !

"I've a bag for meal, and a bag for malt,
    And a bag for barley and corn ;
A bag for bread, and a bag for beef,
    And a bag for my little small horn.

"I have a horn in my pocket,
    I got it from Robin Hood,
And still when I set it to my mouth,
    For thee it blows little good."

"O, wind thy horn, thou proud fellow,
    Of thee I have no doubt.
I wish that thou give such a blast,
    Till both thy eyes fall out."

The first loud blast that he did blow,
    He blew both loud and shrill ;
A hundred and fifty of Robin Hood's men
    Came riding over the hill.

The next loud blast that he did give,
  He blew both loud and amain,
And quickly sixty of Robin Hood's men
  Came shining over the plain.

"O, who are these," the sheriff he said,
  "Come tripping over the lee?"
"They're my attendants," brave Robin did say;
  "They'll pay a visit to thee."

They took the gallows from the slack,
  They set it in the glen,
They hanged the proud sheriff on that,
  Released their own three men.

ROBIN HOOD AND ALLIN A DALE.

Come listen to me, you gallants so free,
  All you that love mirth for to hear,
And I will tell you of a bold outlaw,
  That lived in Nottinghamshire.

As Robin Hood in the forest stood,
  All under the green-wood tree,
There he was aware of a brave young man,
  As fine as fine might be.

The youngster was cloathed in scarlet red,
  In scarlet fine and gay;
And he did frisk it over the plain,
  And chanted a roundelay.

As Robin Hood next morning stood,
  Amongst the leaves so gay,
There did he espy the same young man
  Come drooping along the way.

The scarlet he wore the day before,
  It was clean cast away;
And at every step he fetcht a sigh,
  " Alack and a well a day ! "

Then stepped forth brave Little John,
  And Midge the miller's son,
Which made the young man bend his bow,
  When as he see them come.

"Stand off, stand off," the young man said,
  " What is your will with me ? "
" You must come before our master straight,
  Under yon green-wood tree."

And when he came bold Robin before,
  Robin askt him courteously,
"O hast thou any money to spare
  For my merry men and me ? "

"I have no money," the young man said,
　"But five shillings and a ring;
　And that I have kept this seven long years,
　　To have it at my wedding.

"Yesterday I should have married a maid,
　But she is now from me tane,
　And chosen to be an old knight's delight,
　　Whereby my poor heart is slain."

"What is thy name?" then said Robin Hood,
　"Come tell me, without any fail:"
"By the faith of my body," then said the young man,
　"My name it is Allin a Dale."

"What wilt thou give me," said Robin Hood,
　"In ready gold or fee,
　To help thee to thy true love again,
　　And deliver her unto thee?"

"I have no money," then quoth the young man,
　"No ready gold nor fee,
　But I will swear upon a book
　　Thy true servant for to be."

"How many miles is it to thy true love?
　Come tell me without any guile:"
"By the faith of my body," then said the young man,
　"It is but five little mile."

Then Robin he hasted over the plain,
  He did neither stint nor lin,
Until he came unto the church,
  Where Allin should keep his wedding.

" What hast thou here ? " the bishop he said,
  " I prithee now tell unto me : "
" I am a bold harper," quoth Robin Hood,
  " And the best in the north country."

" O welcome, O welcome," the bishop he said,
  " That musick best pleaseth me ; "
" You shall have no musick," quoth Robin Hood,
  " Till the bride and the bridegroom I see."

With that came in a wealthy knight,
  Which was both grave and old,
And after him a finikin lass,
  Did shine like the glistering gold.

" This is not a fit match," quoth bold Robin Hood,
  " That you do seem to make here ;
For since we are come into the church,
  The bride shall chuse her own dear."

Then Robin Hood put his horn to his mouth,
  And blew blasts two or three ;
When four and twenty bowmen bold
  Came leaping over the lee.

And when they came into the church-yard,
  Marching all on a row,
The first man was Allin a Dale,
  To give bold Robin his bow.

"This is thy true love," Robin he said,
  "Young Allin, as I hear say;
And you shall be married at this same time,
  Before we depart away."

"That shall not be," the bishop he said,
  "For thy word shall not stand;
They shall be three times askt in the church,
  As the law is of our land."

Robin Hood pulld off the bishop's coat,
  And put it upon Little John;
"By the faith of my body," then Robin said,
  "This cloath does make thee a man."

When Little John went into the quire,
  The people began for to laugh;
He askt them seven times in the church,
  Lest three times should not be enough.

"Who gives me this maid?" then said Little John;
  Quoth Robin Hood, "That do I,
And he that takes her from Allin a Dale
  Full dearly he shall her buy."

And thus having ende of this merry wedding,
   The bride lookt like a queen,
And so they returned to the merry green-wood,
   Amongst the leaves so green.

ROBIN HOOD'S DEATH AND BURIAL.

WHEN Robin Hood and Little John,
   Down a down, a down, a down,
   Went o'er yon bank of broom,
Said Robin Hood to Little John,
   "We have shot for many a pound:"
   Hey down, a down, a down.

"But I am not able to shoot one shot more,
   My arrows will not flee;
But I have a cousin lives down below,
   Please God, she will bleed me."

Now Robin is to fair Kirkley gone,
   As fast as he can win;
But before he came there, as we do hear,
   He was taken very ill.

And when that he came to fair Kirkley-hall,
   He knocked all at the ring,
But none was so ready as his cousin hersel
   For to let bold Robin in.

"Will you please to sit down, cousin Robin," she said
  "And drink some beer with me?"
"No, I will neither eat nor drink,
  Till I am blooded by thee."

"Well, I have a room, cousin Robin," she said,
  "Which you did never see,
And if you please to walk therein,
  You blooded by me shall be."

She took him by the lily-white hand,
  And led him to a private room,
And there she blooded bold Robin Hood,
  Whilst one drop of blood would run.

She blooded him in the vein of the arm,
  And locked him up in the room;
There did he bleed all the livelong day,
  Untilt the next day at noon.

He then bethought him of a casement door,
  Thinking for to be gone;
He was so weak he could not leap,
  Nor he could not get down.

He then bethought him of his bugle-horn,
  Which hung low down to his knee;
He set his horn unto his mouth,
  And blew out weak blasts three.

Then Little John, when hearing him,
    As he sat under the tree,
"I fear my master is near dead,
    He blows so wearily."

Then Little John to fair Kirkley is gone,
    As fast as he can dri'e ;
But when he came to Kirkley-hall,
    He broke locks two or three :

Untilt he came bold Robin to,
    Then he fell on his knee :
"A boon, a boon," cries Little John,
    "Master, I beg of thee."

"What is that boon," quoth Robin Hood,
    "Little John, thou begs of me ?"
"It is to burn fair Kirkley-hall,
    And all their nunnery."

"Now nay, now nay," quoth Robin Hood,
    "That boon I'll not grant thee ;
I never hurt woman in all my life,
    Nor man in woman's company.

"I never hurt fair maid in all my time,
    Nor at my end shall it be ;
But give me my bent bow in my hand,
    And a broad arrow I'll let flee ;
And where this arrow is taken up,
    There shall my grave digg'd be.

" Lay me a green sod under my head,
    And another at my feet ;
And lay my bent bow by my side,
    Which was my music sweet ;
And make my grave of gravel and green,
    Which is most right and meet.

" Let me have length and breadth enough,
    With under my head a green sod ;
That they may say, when I am dead,
    Here lies bold Robin Hood."

These words they readily promised him,
    Which did bold Robin please ;
And there they buried bold Robin Hood,
    Near to the fair Kirklèys.

ROMANTIC AND DOMESTIC BALLADS.

ROMANTIC AND DOMESTIC BALLADS.

ANNIE OF LOCHROYAN.

"O wha will shoe my bonny feet?
　　Or wha will glove my hand?
Or wha will lace my middle jimp,
　　Wi' a new-made London band?

"And wha will kame my yellow hair,
　　Wi' a new-made siller kame?
And wha will be my bairn's father,
　　Till love Gregory come hame?"

"Your father'll shoe your bonny feet,
　　Your mother glove your hand;
Your sister lace your middle jimp,
　　Wi' a new-made London band;

"Mysel' will kame your yellow hair
　　Wi' a new-made siller kame;
And the Lord will be the bairn's father
　　Till Gregory come hame."

"O gin I had a bonny ship,
　　And men to sail wi' me,
It's I wad gang to my true love,
　　Sin' he winna come to me!"

Her father's gi'en her a bonny ship,
    And sent her to the strand;
She's ta'en her young son in her arms,
    And turn'd her back to land.

She hadna been on the sea sailing,
    About a month or more,
Till landed has she her bonny ship,
    Near to her true love's door.

The night was dark, an' the wind was cauld,
    And her love was fast asleep,
And the bairn that was in her twa arms,
    Fu' sair began to greet.

Lang stood she at her true love's door,
    And lang tirl'd at the pin;
At length up gat his fause mother,
    Says, "Wha's that wad be in?"

"O it is Annie of Lochroyan,
    Your love, come o'er the sea,
But and your young son in her arms,
    Sae open the door to me."

"Awa, awa, ye ill woman,
    Ye're nae come here for gude;
Ye're but a witch, or a vile warlock,
    Or mermaiden o' the flood!"

"I'm nae a witch, nor vile warlock,
    Nor mermaiden," said she;
"But I am Annie of Lochroyan;
    O open the door to me!"

"O gin ye be Annie of Lochroyan,
    As I trow not you be,
Now tell me some o' the love-tokens
    That pass'd 'tween thee and me."

"O dinna ye mind, love Gregory,
    When we sate at the wine,
How we chang'd the napkins frae our necks,
    It's no sae lang sinsyne?

"And yours was gude, and gude eneugh,
    But nae sae gude as mine;
For yours was o' the cambrick clear,
    But mine o' the silk sae fine.

"And dinna ye mind, love Gregory,
    As we twa sate at dine,
How we chang'd the rings frae our fingers,
    And I can show thee thine?

"And yours was gude, and gude eneugh,
    Yet nae sae gude as mine;
For yours was o' the gude red gold,
    But mine o' the diamonds fine.

"Sae open the door, love Gregory,
  And open it wi' speed;
Or your young son, that is in my arms,
  For cauld will soon be dead!"

"Awa, awa, ye ill woman,
  Gae frae my door for shame;
For I hae gotten anither fair love,
  Sae ye may hie ye hame!"

"O hae ye gotten anither fair love,
  For a' the oaths ye sware?
Then fare ye weel, fause Gregory,
  For me ye'se never see mair!"

O hooly, hooly gaed she back,
  As the day began to peep;
She set her foot on gude ship board,
  And sair, sair did she weep.

"Tak down, tak down that mast o' gowd,
  Set up the mast o' tree;
Ill sets it a forsaken lady
  To sail sae gallantlie!"

Love Gregory started frae his sleep,
  And to his mother did say;
"I dream'd a dream this night, mither,
  That maks my heart right wae.

"I dream'd that Annie of Lochroyan,
  The flower of a' her kin,
Was standing mournin' at my door,
  But nane wad let her in."

"Gin it be for Annie of Lochroyan,
  That ye mak a' this din;
She stood a' last night at your door,
  But I trow she wan na in!"

"O wae betide ye, ill woman!
  An ill deid may ye die,
That wadna open the door to her,
  Nor yet wad waken me!"

O quickly, quickly raise he up,
  And fast ran to the strand;
And then he saw her, fair Annie,
  Was sailing frae the land.

And it's "Hey Annie!" and "How Annie!
  O Annie, winna ye bide?"
But aye the mair that he cried "Annie!"
  The faster ran the tide.

And it's "Hey Annie!" and "How Annie!
  O Annie, speak to me!"
But aye the louder that he cried "Annie!"
  The higher raise the sea.

The wind grew loud, and the sea grew rough,
   And the ship was rent in twain ;
And soon he saw her, fair Annie,
   Come floating through the faem.

He saw his young son in her arms,
   Baith toss'd abune the tide ;
He wrang his hands, and fast he ran,
   And plunged in the sea sae wide.

He catch'd her by the yellow hair,
   And drew her to the strand ;
But cauld and stiff was every limb,
   Afore he reach'd the land.

O first he kiss'd her cherry cheek,
   And syne he kiss'd her chin,
And sair he kiss'd her bonny lips,
   But there was nae breath within.

And he has mourn'd o'er fair Annie,
   Till the sun was ganging down,
Syne wi' a sigh his heart it brast,
   And his soul to heaven has flown.

LORD THOMAS AND FAIR ANNET.

Lord Thomas and fair Annet
　　Sat a' day on a hill,
When night was come, and the sun was set,
　　They had na talk'd their fill.

Lord Thomas said a word in jest,
　　Fair Annet took it ill;
"O I will never wed a wife,
　　Against my ain friends' will."

"Gif ye will never wed a wife,
　　A wife will ne'er wed ye."
Sae he is hame to tell his mither,
　　And kneel'd upon his knee.

"O rede, O rede, mither," he says,
　　"A gude rede gie to me;
O sall I tak' the nut-brown bride,
　　And let fair Annet be?"

"The nut-brown bride has gowd and gear,
　　Fair Annet she's gat nane,
And the little beauty fair Annet has,
　　O it will soon be gane."

And he has to his brither gane;
 "Now, brither, rede ye me,
O sall I marry the nut-brown bride,
 And let fair Annet be ? "

" The nut-brown bride has owsen, brither,
 The nut-brown bride has kye;
I wad hae you marry the nut-brown bride,
 And cast fair Annet by."

" Her owsen may dee in the house, billie,
 And her kye into the byre,
And I sall hae naething to mysel,
 But a fat fadge by the fire."

And he has to his sister gane;
 " Now, sister, rede to me;
O sall I marry the nut-brown bride,
 And set fair Annet free ? "

" I'se rede ye tak' fair Annet, Thomas,
 And let the brown bride alane,
Lest ye sould sigh, and say, Alace,
 What is this we brought hame ? "

" No ! I will tak' my mither's counsel,
 And marry me out o' hand;
And I will tak' the nut-brown bride,
 Fair Annet may leave the land."

Up then rose fair Annet's father,
    Twa hours or it were day,
And he has gane into the bower,
    Wherein fair Annet lay.

" Rise up, rise up, fair Annet," he says,
    "Put on your silken sheen,
Let us gae to Saint Marie's kirk,
    And see that rich weddin'."

" My maids, gae to my dressing-room
    And dress to me my hair,
Where'er ye laid a plait before,
    See ye lay ten times mair.

' My maids, gae to my dressing-room
    And dress to me my smock,
The ae half is o' the holland fine,
    The ither o' needle-work."

The horse fair Annet rade upon,
    He amblit like the wind,
Wi' siller he was shod before,
    Wi' burning gowd behind.

Four-and-twenty siller bells,
    Were a' tied to his mane,
Wi' ae tift o' the norlan' wind,
    They tinkled ane by ane.

Four-and-twenty gay gude knights,
    Rade by fair Annet's side,
And four-and-twenty fair ladies,
    As gin she had been a bride.

And when she cam' to Marie's kirk,
    She sat on Marie's stane;
The cleiding that fair Annet had on,
    It skinkled in their e'en.

And when she cam' into the kirk,
    She skimmer'd like the sun;
The belt that was about her waist,
    Was a' wi' pearls bedone.

She sat her by the nut-brown bride,
    And her e'en they were sae clear,
Lord Thomas he clean forgot the bride,
    When fair Annet drew near.

He had a rose into his hand,
    He gave it kisses three,
And reaching by the nut-brown bride,
    Laid it on Annet's knee.

Up then spak' the nut-brown bride,
    She spak' wi' meikle spite;
" Where gat ye that rose-water, Annet,
    That does mak' ye sae white ? "

"O I did get the rose-water,
    Where ye'll get never nane,
For I did get that rose-water,
    Before that I was born.

"Where I did get that rose-water,
    Ye'll never get the like;
For ye've been washed in Dunnie's well,
    And dried on Dunnie's dyke.

"Tak' up and wear your rose, Thomas,
    And wear't wi' meikle care;
For the woman sall never bear a son
    That will mak' my heart sae sair."

When night was come, and day was gane,
    And a' men boune to bed,
Lord Thomas and the nut-brown bride
    In their chamber were laid.

They were na weel lyen down,
    And scarcely fa'en asleep,
When up and stands she, fair Annet,
    Just at Lord Thomas' feet.

"Weel bruik ye o' your nut-brown bride,
    Between ye and the wa';
And sae will I o' my winding-sheet,
    That suits me best of a'.

"Weel bruik ye o' your nut-brown bride,
  Between ye and the stock;
And sae will I o' my black, black kist,
  That has neither key nor lock!"

Lord Thomas rase, put on his claes,
  Drew till him hose and shoon;
And he is to fair Annet's bower,
  By the lee light o' the moon.

The firsten bower that he cam' till,
  There was right dowie wark;
Her mither and her three sisters,
  Were making fair Annet a sark.

The nexten bower that he cam' till,
  There was right dowie cheer;
Her father and her seven brethren,
  Were making fair Annet a bier.

The lasten bower that he cam' till,
  O heavy was his care,
The deid candles were burning bright,
  Fair Annet was streekit there.

"O I will kiss your cheek, Annet,
  And I will kiss your chin;
And I will kiss your clay-cauld lip,
  But I'll ne'er kiss woman again.

" This day ye deal at Annet's wake,
　　The bread but and the wine ;
Before the morn at twal' o'clock,
　　They'll deal the same at mine."

The tane was buried in Marie's kirk,
　　The tither in Marie's quire,
And out o' the tane there grew a birk,
　　And out o' the tither a brier.

And ay they grew, and ay they drew,
　　Until they twa did meet,
And every ane that pass'd them by,
　　Said, " Thae's been lovers sweet ! "

———————

THE BANKS O' YARROW.

LATE at e'en, drinking the wine,
　　And ere they paid the lawing,
They set a combat them between,
　　To fight it in the dawing.

" What though ye be my sister's lord,
　　We'll cross our swords to-morrow."
" What though my wife your sister be,
　　I'll meet ye then on Yarrow."

"O stay at hame, my ain gude lord!
    O stay, my ain dear marrow!
My cruel brither will you betray
    On the dowie banks o' Yarrow."

"O fare ye weel, my lady dear!
    And put aside your sorrow;
For if I gae, I'll sune return
    Frae the bonny banks o' Yarrow."

She kiss'd his cheek, she kaim'd his hair,
    As oft she'd dune before, O;
She belted him wi' his gude brand,
    And he's awa' to Yarrow.

When he gaed up the Tennies bank,
    As he gaed mony a morrow,
Nine armed men lay in a den,
    On the dowie braes o' Yarrow.

"O come ye here to hunt or hawk
    The bonny Forest thorough?
Or come ye here to wield your brand
    Upon the banks o' Yarrow?"

"I come not here to hunt or hawk,
    As oft I've dune before, O,
But I come here to wield my brand
    Upon the banks o' Yarrow.

"If ye attack me nine to ane,
 Then may God send ye sorrow!—
Yet will I fight while stand I may,
 On the bonny banks o' Yarrow."

Two has he hurt, and three has slain,
 On the bloody braes o' Yarrow;
But the stubborn knight crept in behind,
 And pierced his body thorough.

"Gae hame, gae hame, you brither John,
 And tell your sister sorrow,—
To come and lift her leafu' lord
 On the dowie banks o' Yarrow."

Her brither John gaed ower yon hill,
 As oft he'd dune before, O;
There he met his sister dear,
 Cam' rinnin' fast to Yarrow.

"I dreamt a dream last night," she says,
 "I wish it binna sorrow;
I dreamt I pu'd the heather green
 Wi' my true love on Yarrow."

"I'll read your dream, sister," he says,
 "I'll read it into sorrow;
Ye're bidden go take up your love,
 He's sleeping sound on Yarrow."

She's torn the ribbons frae her head
    That were baith braid and narrow;
She's kilted up her lang claithing,
    And she's awa' to Yarrow.

She's ta'en him in her arms twa,
    And gien him kisses thorough;
She sought to bind his mony wounds,
    But he lay dead on Yarrow.

"O haud your tongue," her father says,
    "And let be a' your sorrow;
I'll wed you to a better lord
    Than him ye lost on Yarrow."

"O haud your tongue, father," she says,
    "Far warse ye mak' my sorrow;
A better lord could never be
    Than him that lies on Yarrow."

She kissed his lips, she kaim'd his hair,
    As oft she'd dune before, O;
And there wi' grief her heart did break
    Upon the banks o' Yarrow.

THE DOUGLAS TRAGEDY.

"Rise up, rise up, now, Lord Douglas," she says,
    "And put on your armour so bright;
Lord William will hae Lady Margret awa
    Before that it be light."

"Rise up, rise up, my seven bold sons,
    And put on your armour so bright,
And take better care of your youngest sister,
    For your eldest's awa the last night."

He's mounted her on a milk-white steed,
    And himself on a dapple gray,
With a bugelet horn hung down by his side,
    And lightly they rode away.

Lord William lookit o'er his left shoulder,
    To see what he could see,
And there he spy'd her seven brethren bold,
    Come riding over the lee.

"Light down, light down, Lady Margret," he said,
    "And hold my steed in your hand,
Until that against your seven brethren bold,
    And your father, I mak' a stand."

She held his steed in her milk-white hand,
  And never shed one tear,
Until that she saw her seven brethren fa',
  And her father hard fighting, who lov'd her so dear.

" O hold your hand, Lord William !" she said,
  " For your strokes they are wondrous sair;
True lovers I can get many a ane,
  But a father I can never get mair."

O she's ta'en out her handkerchief,
  It was o' the holland sae fine,
And aye she dighted her father's bloody wounds,
  That were redder than the wine.

"O chuse, O chuse, Lady Margret," he said,
  " O whether will ye gang or bide ? "
" I'll gang, I'll gang, Lord William," she said,
  " For ye have left me nae other guide."

He's lifted her on a milk-white steed,
  And himself on a dapple gray,
With a bugelet horn hung down by his side,
  And slowly they baith rade away.

O they rade on, and on they rade,
  And a' by the light of the moon,
Until they came to yon wan water,
  And there they lighted down.

They lighted down to tak' a drink
   Of the spring that ran sae clear,
And down the stream ran his gude heart's blood,
   And sair she gan to fear.

"Hold up, hold up, Lord William," she says,
   "For I fear that you are slain;"
"'Tis naething but the shadow of my scarlet cloak,
   That shines in the water sae plain."

O they rade on, and on they rade,
   And a' by the light of the moon,
Until they cam' to his mother's ha' door,
   And there they lighted down.

"Get up, get up, lady mother," he says,
   "Get up, and let me in!
Get up, get up, lady mother," he says,
   "For this night my fair lady I've win.

"O mak' my bed, lady mother," he says,
   "O mak' it braid and deep,
And lay Lady Margret close at my back,
   And the sounder I will sleep."

Lord William was dead lang ere midnight,
   Lady Margret lang ere day,
And all true lovers that go thegither,
   May they have mair luck than they!

Lord William was buried in St. Mary's kirk,
    Lady Margret in Mary's quire;
Out o' the lady's grave grew a bonny red rose,
    And out o' the knight's a briar.

And they twa met, and they twa plat,
    And fain they wad be near;
And a' the warld might ken right weel
    They were twa lovers dear.

But by and rade the Black Douglas,
    And wow but he was rough!
For he pull'd up the bonny briar,
    And flang't in St. Mary's Loch.

FINE FLOWERS I' THE VALLEY.

THERE were three sisters in a ha',
    (Fine flowers i' the valley;)
There came three lords amang them a',
    (The red, green, and the yellow.)

The first o' them was clad in red,
    (Fine flowers i' the valley;)
"O lady, will ye be my bride?"
    (Wi' the red, green, and the yellow.)

The second o' them was clad in green,
    (Fine flowers i' the valley ;)
"O lady, will ye be my queen ? "
    (Wi' the red, green, and the yellow.)

The third o' them was clad in yellow,
    (Fine flowers i' the valley ;)
"O lady, will ye be my marrow ? "
    (Wi' the red, green, and the yellow.)

"O ye maun ask my father dear,
    (Fine flowers i' the valley ;)
Likewise the mother that did me bear ; "
    (Wi' the red, green, and the yellow.)

"And ye maun ask my sister Ann,
    (Fine flowers i' the valley ;)
And not forget my brother John ; "
    (Wi' the red, green, and the yellow.)

"O I have ask'd thy father dear,
    (Fine flowers i' the valley ;)
Likewise the mother that did thee bear ; "
    (Wi' the red, green, and the yellow.)

"And I have ask'd your sister Ann,
    (Fine flowers i' the valley ;)
But I forgot your brother John ; "
    (Wi' the red, green, and the yellow.)

Now when the wedding day was come,
   (Fine flowers i' the valley ;)
The knight would take his bonny bride home,
   (Wi' the red, green, and the yellow.)

And mony a lord, and mony a knight,
   (Fine flowers i' the valley ;)
Cam' to behold that lady bright,
   (Wi' the red, green, and the yellow.)

There was nae man that did her see,
   (Fine flowers i' the valley ;)
But wished himsell bridegroom to be,
   (Wi' the red, green, and the yellow.)

Her father led her down the stair,
   (Fine flowers i' the valley ;)
And her sisters twain they kiss'd her there ;
   (Wi' the red, green, and the yellow.)

Her mother led her through the close,
   (Fine flowers i' the valley ;)
Her brother John set her on her horse ;
   (Wi' the red, green, and the yellow.)

"You are high, and I am low,
   (Fine flowers i' the valley ;)
Give me a kiss before you go,"
   (Wi' the red, green, and the yellow.)

She was louting down to kiss him sweet,
  (Fine flowers i' the valley;)
When wi' his knife he wounded her deep,
  (Wi' the red, green, and the yellow.)

She hadna ridden through half the town,
  (Fine flowers i' the valley;)
Until her heart's blood stained her gown,
  (Wi' the red, green, and the yellow.)

"Ride saftly on," said the best young man,
  (Fine flowers i' the valley;)
"I think our bride looks pale and wan!"
  (Wi' the red, green, and the yellow.)

"O lead me over into yon stile,
  (Fine flowers i' the valley;)
That I may stop and breathe awhile,"
  (Wi' the red, green, and the yellow.)

"O lead me over into yon stair,
  (Fine flowers i' the valley;)
For there I'll lie and bleed nae mair,"
  (Wi' the red, green, and the yellow.)

"O what will you leave to your father dear?"
  (Fine flowers i' the valley;)
"The siller-shod steed that brought me here,"
  (Wi' the red, green, and the yellow.)

"What will you leave to your mother dear?"
　(Fine flowers i' the valley;)
"My wedding shift which I do wear,"
　(Wi' the red, green, and the yellow.)

"But she must wash it very clean,
　(Fine flowers i' the valley;)
For my heart's blood sticks in every seam."
　(Wi' the red, green, and the yellow.)

"What will you leave to your sister Ann?"
　(Fine flowers i' the valley;)
"My silken gown that stands its lane,"
　(Wi' the red, green, and the yellow.)

"And what will you leave to your brother John?"
　(Fine flowers i' the valley;)
"The gates o' hell to let him in,"
　(Wi' the red, green, and the yellow.)

THE GAY GOSS–HAWK.

"O WELL is me, my gay goss-hawk,
　That ye can speak and flee;
For ye shall carry a love-letter
　To my true-love frae me.

"O how shall I your true-love find,
　Or how should I her knaw?
I bear a tongue ne'er wi' her spake,
　An eye that ne'er her saw."

"O well shall you my true-love ken,
    Sae soon as her ye see,
For of a' the flowers o' fair England,
    The fairest flower is she.

" And when ye come to her castle,
    Light on the bush of ash,
And sit ye there, and sing our loves,
    As she comes frae the mass.

" And when she goes into the house,
    Light ye upon the whin ;
And sit ye there, and sing our loves,
    As she gaes out and in."

Lord William has written a love-letter,
    Put in under the wing sae grey ;
And the bird is awa' to southern land,
    As fast as he could gae.

And when he flew to that castle,
    He lighted on the ash,
And there he sat, and sang their loves,
    As she came frae the mass.

And when she went into the house,
    He flew unto the whin ;
And there he sat, and sang their loves,
    As she gaed out and in.

"Feast on, feast on, my maidens a',
　　The wine flows you amang,
Till I gae to the west-window,
　　And hear a birdie's sang."

She's gane into the west-window,
　　And fainly aye it drew,
And soon into her white silk lap
　　The bird the letter threw.

"Ye're bidden send your love a send,
　　For he has sent you three ;
And tell him where he can see you,
　　Or for your love he'll die."

"I send him the rings from my white fingers,
　　The garlands aff my hair,
I send him the heart that's in my breast,
　　What would my love hae mair ?
And at the fourth kirk in fair Scotland,
　　Ye'll bid him meet me there."

She's gane until her father dear,
　　As fast as she could hie,
"An asking, an asking, my father dear,
　　An asking grant ye me !
That if I die in merry England,
　　In Scotland you'll bury me.

" At the first kirk o' fair Scotland,
  Ye'll cause the bells be rung ;
At the neist kirk o' fair Scotland
  Ye'll cause the mass be sung.

" At the third kirk o' fair Scotland,
  Ye'll deal the gowd for me ;
At the fourth kirk o' fair Scotland,
  It's there you'll bury me."

She has ta'en her to her bigly bower,
  As fast as she could hie ;
And she has drappèd down like deid,
  Beside her mother's knee ;
Then out and spak' an auld witch-wife,
  By the fire-side sate she.

Says, — " Drap the het lead on her cheek,
  And drap it on her chin,
And drap it on her rose-red lips,
  And she will speak again ;
O meikle will a maiden do,
  To her true love to win ! "

They drapt the het lead on her cheek,
  They drapt it on her chin,
They drapt it on her rose-red lips,
  But breath was nane within.

Then up arose her seven brothers,
    And made for her a bier;
The boards were of the cedar wood,
    The plates o' silver clear.

And up arose her seven sisters,
    And made for her a sark;
The claith of it was satin fine,
    The steeking silken wark.

The first Scots kirk that they cam' to,
    They gar'd the bells be rung;
The neist Scots kirk that they cam' to,
    They gar'd the mass be sung.

The third Scots kirk that they cam' to,
    They dealt the gowd for her;
The fourth Scots kirk that they cam' to,
    Her true-love met them there.

"Set down, set down the bier," he quoth,
    Till I look on the dead;
The last time that I saw her face,
    Her cheeks were rosy red."

He rent the sheet upon her face,
    A little abune the chin;
And fast he saw her colour come,
    And sweet she smiled on him.

"O give me a chive of your bread, my love,
  And ae drap o' your wine ;
For I have fasted for your sake,
  These weary lang days nine !

"Gae hame, gae hame, my seven brothers ;
  Gae hame an' blaw your horn !
I trow ye wad hae gi'en me the skaith,
  But I've gi'ed you the scorn.

"I cam' not here to fair Scotland,
  To lie amang the dead ;
But I cam' here to fair Scotland,
  Wi' my ain true-love to wed."

YOUNG REDIN.

FAIR Catherine from her bower-window
  Looked over heath and wood ;
She heard a smit o' bridle-reins,
  And the sound did her heart good.

"Welcome, young Redin, welcome !
  And welcome again, my dear !
Light down, light down from your horse," she says,
  "It's long since you were here."

"O gude morrow, lady, gude morrow, lady;
    God mak' you safe and free !
I'm come to tak' my last fareweel,
    And pay my last visit to thee.

"I mustna light, and I canna light,
    I winna stay at a';
For a fairer lady than ten of thee
    Is waiting at Castleswa'."

"O if your love be changed, my dear,
    Since better may not be,
Yet, ne'ertheless, for auld lang syne,
    Bide this ae night wi' me."

She birl'd him wi' the ale and wine,
    As they sat down to sup;
A living man he laid him down,
    But I wot he ne'er rose up.

"Now lie ye there, young Redin," she says,
    "O lie ye there till morn, —
Though a fairer lady than ten of me
    Is waiting till you come home !

"O lang, lang is the winter night,
    Till day begins to daw ;
There is a dead man in my bower,
    And I would he were awa'."

She cried upon her bower-maiden,
　　Aye ready at her ca':
"There is a knight into my bower,
　　'Tis time he were awa'."

They've booted him and spurred him,
　　As he was wont to ride,
A hunting-horn tied round his waist,
　　A sharp sword by his side;
And they've flung him into the wan water,
　　The deepest pool in Clyde.

Then up bespake a little bird
　　That sate upon the tree,
"Gae hame, gae hame, ye fause lady,
　　And pay your maid her fee."

"Come down, come down, my pretty bird,
　　That sits upon the tree;
I have a cage of beaten gold,
　　I'll gie it unto thee."

"Gae hame, gae hame, ye fause lady;
　　I winna come down to thee;
For as ye have done to young Redin,
　　Ye'd do the like to me."

O there came seeking young Redin
　　Mony a lord and knight,
And there came seeking young Redin
　　Mony a lady bright.

They've called on Lady Catherine,
　　But she sware by oak and thorn
That she saw him not, young Redin,
　　Since yesterday at morn.

The lady turned her round about,
　　Wi' mickle mournfu' din :
" It fears me sair o' Clyde water
　　That he is drowned therein."

Then up spake young Redin's mither,
　　The while she made her mane :
" My son kenn'd a' the fords o' Clyde,
　　He'd ride them ane by ane."

" Gar douk, gar douk ! " his father he cried,
　　" Gar douk for gold and fee !
O wha will douk for young Redin's sake,
　　And wha will douk for me ? "

They hae douked in at ae weil-head,
　　And out again at the ither :
" We'll douk nae mair for young Redin,
　　Although he were our brither."

Then out it spake a little bird
　　That sate upon the spray :
" What gars ye seek him, young Redin,
　　Sae early in the day ?

"Leave aff your douking on the day,
    And douk at dark o' night;
Aboon the pool young Redin lies in,
    The candles they'll burn bright."

They left aff their douking on the day,
    They hae douked at dark o' night;
Aboon the pool where young Redin lay,
    The candles they burned bright.

The deepest pool in a' the stream
    They found young Redin in;
Wi' a great stone tied across his breast
    To keep his body down.

Then up and spake the little bird,
    Says, "What needs a' this din?
It was Lady Catherine took his life,
    And hided him in the linn."

She sware her by the sun and moon,
    She sware by grass and corn,
She hadna seen him, young Redin,
    Since Monanday at morn.

"It's surely been my bower-woman, —
    O ill may her betide!
I ne'er wad hae slain my young Redin,
    And thrown him in the Clyde."

Now they hae cut baith fern and thorn,
  The bower-woman to brin;
And they hae made a big balefire,
  And put this maiden in;
But the fire it took na on her cheek,
  It took na on her chin.

Out they hae ta'en the bower-woman,
  And put her mistress in;
The flame took fast upon her cheek,
  Took fast upon her chin,
Took fast upon her fair bodie,
  Because of her deadly sin.

WILLIE AND MAY MARGARET.

WILLIE stands in his stable,
  A-clapping of his steed;
And over his white fingers
  His nose began to bleed.

"Gie corn to my horse, mither;
  Gie meat unto my man;
For I maun gang to Margaret's bower,
  Before the night comes on."

"O stay at home, my son Willie!
  The wind blaws cold and stour;
The night will be baith mirk and late,
  Before ye reach her bower."

"O tho' the night were ever sae dark,
    O the wind blew never sae cauld,
I will be in May Margaret's bower
    Before twa hours be tauld."

"O bide this night wi' me, Willie,
    O bide this night wi' me !
The bestan fowl in a' the roost
    At your supper, my son, shall be."

"A' your fowls, and a' your roosts,
    I value not a pin ;
I only care for May Margaret ;
    And ere night to her bower I'll win."

"O an ye gang to May Margaret
    Sae sair against my will,
In the deepest pot o' Clyde's water
    My malison ye's feel !"

He mounted on his coal-black steed,
    And fast he rade awa' ;
But ere he came to Clyde's water
    Fu' loud the wind did blaw.

As he rade over yon hie hie hill,
    And doun yon dowie den,
There was a roar in Clyde's water
    Wad feared a hundred men.

But Willie has swam through Clyde's water,
    Though it was wide and deep;
And he came to May Margaret's door
    When a' were fast asleep.

O he's gane round and round about,
    And tirled at the pin,
But doors were steeked and windows barred,
    And nane to let him in.

"O open the door to me, Margaret!
    O open and let me in!
For my boots are fu' o' Clyde's water,
    And frozen to the brim."

"I daurna open the door to you,
    I daurna let you in;
For my mither she is fast asleep,
    And I maun mak' nae din."

"O gin ye winna open the door,
    Nor be sae kind to me,
Now tell me o' some out-chamber,
    Where I this night may be."

"Ye canna win in this night, Willie,
    Nor here ye canna be;
For I've nae chambers out nor in,
    Nae ane but barely three.

" The tane is fu' to the roof wi' corn,
 The tither is fu' wi' hay ;
The third is fu' o' merry young men,
 They winna remove till day."

" O fare ye weel, then, May Margaret,
 Sin' better it manna be.
I have won my mither's malison,
 Coming this night to thee."

He's mounted on his coal-black steed,
 O but his heart was wae !
But e'er he came to Clyde's water,
 'Twas half-way up the brae.

When down he rade to the river-flood,
 'Twas fast flowing ower the brim ;
The rushing that was in Clyde's water
 Took Willie's rod frae him.

He leaned him ower his saddle-bow
 To catch his rod again ;
The rushing that was in Clyde's water
 Took Willie's hat frae him.

He leaned him ower his saddle-bow
 To catch his hat by force ;
The rushing that was in Clyde's water
 Took Willie frae his horse.

"O I canna turn my horse's head ;
  I canna strive to sowm ;
I've gotten my mither's malison,
  And it's here that I maun drown !"

The very hour this young man sank
  Into the pot sae deep,
Up wakened his love, May Margaret,
  Out of her heavy sleep.

"Come hither, come hither, my minnie dear,
  Come hither read my dream ;
I dreamed my love Willie was at our gates,
  And nane wad let him in."

"Lie still, lie still, dear Margaret,
  Lie still and tak' your rest ;
Your lover Willie was at the gates,
  'Tis but two quarters past."

Nimbly, nimbly rase she up,
  And quickly put she on ;
While ever against her window
  The louder blew the win'.

Out she ran into the night,
  And down the dowie den ;
The strength that was in Clyde's water
  Wad drown five hundred men.

She stepped in to her ankle,
    She stepped free and bold;
"Ohone, alas!" said that ladye,
    "This water is wondrous cold."

The second step that she waded,
    She waded to the knee;
Says she, "I'd fain wade farther in,
    If I my love could see."

The neistan step that she waded,
    She waded to the chin;
'Twas a whirlin' pot o' Clyde's water
    She got sweet Willie in.

"O ye've had a cruel mither, Willie!
    And I have had anither;
Bnt we shall sleep in Clyde's water
    Like sister and like brither."

YOUNG BEICHAN.

In London was young Beichan born,
    He longed strange countries for to see,
But he was ta'en by a savage Moor,
    Who handled him right cruellie.

For he viewed the fashions of that land,
    Their way of worship viewèd he,
But to Mahound or Termagant
    Would Beichan never bend a knee.

So in every shoulder they've putten a bore,
　In every bore they've putten a tree,
And they have made him trail the wine
　And spices on his fair bodie.

They've casten him in a dungeon deep,
　Where he could neither hear nor see,
For seven years they've kept him there,
　Till he for hunger's like to dee.

This Moor he had but ae daughter,
　Her name was callèd Susie Pye,
And every day as she took the air,
　Near Beichan's prison she passed by.

And so it fell upon a day,
　About the middle time of Spring,
As she was passing by that way,
　She heard young Beichan sadly sing.

All night long no rest she got,
　Young Beichan's song for thinking on;
She's stown the keys from her father's head,
　And to the prison strang is gone.

And she has opened the prison doors,
　I wot she opened two or three,
Ere she could come young Beichan at,
　He was locked up so curiouslie.

But when she cam' young Beichan till,
   Sore wondered he that may to see;
He took her for some fair captive:
   "Fair lady, I pray, of what countrie?"

"O have ye any lands," she said,
   "Or castles in your own countrie,
That ye could give to a lady fair,
   From prison strang to set you free?"

"Near London town I have a hall,
   And other castles two or three;
I'll give them all to the lady fair
   That out of prison will set me free."

"Give me the truth of your right hand,
   The truth of it give unto me,
That for seven years ye'll no lady wed,
   Unless it be alang with me."

"I'll give thee the truth of my right hand,
   The truth of it I'll freely gie,
That for seven years I'll stay unwed,
   For the kindness thou dost show to me."

And she has brib'd the proud warder,
   Wi' mickle gold and white monie,
She's gotten the keys of the prison strang,
   And she has set young Beichan free.

She's gi'en him to eat the good spice-cake,
    She's gi'en him to drink the blude-red wine,
She's bidden him sometimes think on her,
    That sae kindly freed him out o' pine.

And she has broken her finger-ring,
    And to Beichan half of it gave she:
"Keep it, to mind you in foreign land
    Of the lady's love that set you free.

"And set your foot on good ship-board,
    And haste ye back to your ain countrie,
And before that seven years have an end,
    Come back again, love, and marry me."

But lang ere seven years had an end,
    She longed full sore her love to see,
So she's set her foot on good ship-board,
    And turned her back on her ain countrie.

She sailèd east, she sailèd west,
    Till to fair England's shore she came,
Where a bonny shepherd she espied,
    Was feeding his sheep upon the plain.

"What news, what news, thou bonny shepherd?
    What news hast thou to tell to me?"
"Such news I hear, ladie," he says,
    "The like was never in this countrie.

"There is a wedding in yonder hall,
    And ever the bells ring merrilie;
It is Lord Beichan's wedding-day
    Wi' a lady fair o' high degree."

She's putten her hand into her pocket,
    Gi'en him the gold and white monie;
"Hay, take ye that, my bonny boy,
    All for the news thou tell'st to me."

When she came to young Beichan's gate,
    She tirlèd saftly at the pin;
So ready was the proud porter
    To open and let this lady in.

"Is this young Beichan's hall," she said,
    "Or is that noble lord within?"
"Yea, he's in the hall among them all,
    And this is the day o' his weddin."

"And has he wed anither love?
    And has he clean forgotten me?"
And sighin said that ladie gay,
    "I wish I were in my ain countrie."

And she has ta'en her gay gold ring
    That with her love she brake sae free;
Says, "Gie him that, ye proud porter,
    And bid the bridegroom speak wi' me."

When the porter came his lord before,
    He kneeled down low upon his knee:
"What aileth thee, my proud porter,
    Thou art so full of courtesie?"

"I've been porter at your gates,
    It's now for thirty years and three;
But the lovely lady that stands thereat,
    The like o' her did I never see.

"For on every finger she has a ring,
    And on her mid-finger she has three,
And meikle gold aboon her brow.
    Sae fair a may did I never see."

It's out then spak the bride's mother,
    And an angry woman, I wot, was she:
"Ye might have excepted our bonny bride,
    And twa or three of our companie."

"O hold your tongue, thou bride's mother,
    Of all your folly let me be;
She's ten times fairer nor the bride,
    And all that's in your companie.

"And this golden ring that's broken in twa,
    This half o' a golden ring sends she:
'Ye'll carry that to Lord Beichan,' she says,
    'And bid him come an' speak wi' me.'

" She begs one sheave of your white bread,
  But and a cup of your red wine,
And to remember the lady's love
  That last relieved you out of pine."

" O well-a-day ! " said Beichan then,
  " That I so soon have married me !
For it can be none but Susie Pye,
  That for my love has sailed the sea."

And quickly hied he down the stair ;
  Of fifteen steps he made but three ;
He's ta'en his bonny love in his arms
  And kist and kist her tenderlie.

" O hae ye ta'en anither bride ?
  And hae ye clean forgotten me ?
And hae ye quite forgotten her
  That gave you life and libertie ? "

She lookit o'er her left shoulder,
  To hide the tears stood in her ee :
" Now fare thee well, young Beichan," she says,
  " I'll try to think no more on thee."

" O never, never, Susie Pye,
  For surely this can never be,
Nor ever shall I wed but her
  That's done and dreed so much for me."

Then out and spak the forenoon bride:
    " My lord, your love it changeth soon.
This morning I was made your bride,
    And another chose ere it be noon."

" O hold thy tongue, thou forenoon bride,
    Ye're ne'er a whit the worse for me,
And whan ye return to your ain land,
    A double dower I'll send with thee."

He's ta'en Susie Pye by the milkwhite hand,
    And led her thro' the halls sae hie,
And aye as he kist her red-rose lips,
    " Ye're dearly welcome, jewel, to me."

He's ta'en her by the milkwhite hand,
    And led her to yon fountain-stane;
He's changed her name from Susie Pye,
    And call'd her his bonny love, Lady Jane.

GILDEROY.

Gilderoy was a bonnie boy,
    Had roses till his shoon,
His stockings were of silken soy,
    Wi' garters hanging doun:
It was, I ween, a comely sight,
    To see sae trim a boy;
He was my joy and heart's delight,
    My winsome Gilderoy.

O sic twa charming e'en he had,
  A breath as sweet as rose,
He never ware a Highland plaid,
  But costly silken clothes ;
He gained the love of ladies gay,
  Nane e'er to him was coy ;
Ah, wae is me ! I mourn this day
  For my dear Gilderoy.

My Gilderoy and I were born
  Baith in one toun together,
We scant were seven years beforn
  We 'gan to luve each ither ;
Our daddies and our mammies they
  Were fill'd wi' meikle joy,
To think upon the bridal day
  Of me and Gilderoy.

For Gilderoy, that luve of mine,
  Gude faith, I freely bought
A wedding sark of Holland fine,
  Wi' dainty ruffles wrought ;
And he gied me a wedding-ring,
  Which I received wi' joy ;
Nae lad nor lassie e'er could sing
  Like me and Gilderoy.

Wi' meikle joy we spent our prime,
  Till we were baith sixteen,
And aft we passed the langsam time
  Amang the leaves sae green ;

Aft on the banks we'd sit us there,
  And sweetly kiss and toy ;
Wi' garlands gay wad deck my hair
  My handsome Gilderoy.

O that he still had been content
  Wi' me to lead his life !
But ah, his manfu' heart was bent
  To stir in feats of strife.
And he in many a venturous deed
  His courage bold wad try ;
And now this gars my heart to bleed
  For my dear Gilderoy.

And when of me his leave he took,
  The tears they wat mine e'e ;
I gied him sic a parting look :
  " My benison gang wi' thee !
God speed thee weel, my ain dear heart,
  For gane is all my joy ;
My heart is rent sith we maun part,
  My handsome Gilderoy."

The Queen of Scots possessèd nought
  That my luve let me want ;
For cow and ewe he to me brought,
  And e'en when they were scant :
All these did honestly possess,
  He never did annoy
Who never failed to pay their cess
  To my luve Gilderoy.

My Gilderoy, baith far and near,
  Was fear'd in every toun,
And bauldly bare awa' the gear
  Of many a lawland loun:
For man to man durst meet him nane,
  He was sae brave a boy;
At length with numbers he was ta'en,
  My winsome Gilderoy.

Wae worth the loun that made the laws,
  To hang a man for gear;
To reive of life for sic a cause,
  As stealing horse or mare!
Had not these laws been made sae strick,
  I ne'er had lost my joy,
Wi' sorrow ne'er had wat my cheek,
  For my dear Gilderoy.

Gif Gilderoy had done amiss,
  He might have banished been.
Ah, what sair cruelty is this,
  To hang sic handsome men!
To hang the flower o' Scottish land,
  Sae sweet and fair a boy!
Nae lady had so white a hand
  As thee, my Gilderoy.

Of Gilderoy sae 'fraid they were,
  They bound him meikle strong,
To Edinburgh they took him there,
  And on a gallows hung:

They hung him high aboon the rest,
 He was sae trim a boy ;
There died the youth whom I lo'ed best,
 My handsome Gilderoy.

Sune as he yielded up his breath,
 I bare his corpse away,
Wi' tears that trickled for his death,
 I wash'd his comely clay ;
And sicker in a grave sae deep
 I laid the dear-lo'ed boy ;
And now forever I maun weep
 My winsome Gilderoy.

BONNY BARBARA ALLAN.

It was in and about the Martinmas time,
 When the green leaves were a falling,
That Sir John Graeme, in the West Country,
 Fell in love with Barbara Allan.

He sent his men down through the town,
 To the place where she was dwelling :
"O haste and come to my master dear,
 Gin ye be Barbara Allan."

O hooly, hooly rose she up,
 To the place where he was lying,
And when she drew the curtain by,
 "Young man, I think you're dying."

"O it's I'm sick, and very, very sick,
　And it's a' for Barbara Allan;"
"O the better for me ye's never be,
　Tho your heart's blood were a spilling.

"O dinna ye mind, young man," said she,
　" When ye was in the tavern a drinking,
That ye made the healths gae round and round,
　And slighted Barbara Allan?"

He turned his face unto the wall,
　And death was with him dealing;
"Adieu, adieu, my dear friends all,
　And be kind to Barbara Allan."

And slowly, slowly raise she up,
　And slowly, slowly left him,
And sighing said, she could not stay,
　Since death of life had reft him.

She had not gane a mile but twa,
　When she heard the dead-bell ringing,
And every jow that the dead-bell gied,
　It cry'd, Woe to Barbara Allan!

"O mother, mother, make my bed!
　O make it saft and narrow!
Since my love died for me to-day,
　I'll die for him to-morrow."

THE GARDENER.

THE gard'ner stands in his bower door,
    Wi' a primrose in his hand,
And by there cam' a leal maiden,
    As jimp as a willow wand.

"O ladie, can ye fancy me,
    For to be my bride?
Ye'se get a' the flowers in my garden,
    To be to you a weed.

"The lily white sall be your smock;
    It becomes your bodie best;
Your head sall be buskt wi' gilly-flower,
    Wi' the primrose in your breast.

"Your goun sall be the sweet-william;
    Your coat the camovine;
Your apron o' the sallads neat,
    That taste baith sweet and fine.

"Your hose sall be the brade kail-blade,
    That is baith brade and lang;
Narrow, narrow at the cute,
    And brade, brade at the brawn.

" Your gloves sall be the marigold,
    All glittering to your hand,
  Weel spread owre wi' the blue blaewort,
    That grows amang corn-land."

" O fare ye weil, young man," she says,
    " Fareweil, and I bid adieu ;
  If you can fancy me," she says,
    " I canna fancy you.

" Sin' ye've provided a weed for me
    Amang the simmer flowers,
  It's I'se provide anither for you,
    Amang the winter-showers :

" The new fawn snaw to be your smock ;
    It becomes your bodie best ;
  Your head sall be wrapt wi' the eastern wind,
    And the cauld rain on your breast."

ETIN THE FORESTER.

LADY MARGARET sits in her bower door,
    Sewing her silken seam ;
  She heard a note in Elmond's wood,
    And wished she there had been.

She loot the seam fa' frae her side,
    And the needle to her tae,
  And she is aff to Elmond's wood
    As fast as she could gae.

She hadna pu'd a nut, a nut,
   Nor broken a branch but ane,
Till by there cam' a young hynd chiel,
   Says, "Lady, lat alane.

"O why pu' ye the nut, the nut,
   Or why brake ye the tree?
For I am forester o' this wood:
   Ye should spier leave at me."

"I'll spier leave at na living man,
   Nor yet will I at thee;
My father is king o'er a' this realm,
   This wood belangs to me."

"You're welcome to the wood, Marg'ret,
   You're welcome here to me;
A fairer bower than e'er you saw.
   I'll bigg this night for thee."

He has bigged a bower beside the thorn
   He has fenced it up wi' stane,
And there within the Elmond wood,
   They twa has dwelt their lane.

He kept her in the Elmond wood,
   For twelve lang years and mair;
And seven fair sons to Hynd Etin,
   Did that gay lady bear.

It fell out ance upon a day,
　　To the hunting he has gane;
And he has ta'en his eldest son,
　　To gang alang wi' him.

When they were in the gay greenwood,
　　They heard the mavis sing;
When they were up aboon the brae,
　　They heard the kirk bells ring.

" O I wad ask ye something, father,
　　An' ye wadna angry be!"
" Say on, say on, my bonny boy,
　　Ye'se nae be quarrell'd by me."

" My mither's cheeks are aft-times weet,
　　It's seldom they are dry;
What is't that gars my mither greet,
　　And sob sae bitterlie?"

" Nae wonder she suld greet, my boy,
　　Nae wonder she suld pine,
For it is twelve lang years and mair,
　　She's seen nor kith nor kin,
And it is twelve lang years and mair,
　　Since to the kirk she's been.

" Your mither was an Earl's daughter,
　　And cam' o' high degree,
And she might hae wedded the first in the land,
　　Had she nae been stown by me.

" For I was but her father's page,
　　And served him on my knee ;
And yet my love was great for her,
　　And sae was hers for me."

" I'll shoot the laverock i' the lift,
　　The buntin on the tree,
And bring them to my mither hame,
　　See if she'll merrier be."

It fell upon anither day,
　　This forester thought lang ;
And he is to the hunting gane
　　The forest leaves amang.

Wi' bow and arrow by his side,
　　He took his path alane ;
And left his seven young children
　　To bide wi' their mither at hame.

" O I wad ask ye something, mither,
　　An ye wadna angry be."
" Ask on, ask on, my eldest son ;
　　Ask ony thing at me."

" Your cheeks are aft-times weet, mither ;
　　You're greetin', as I can see."
" Nae wonder, nae wonder, my little son,
　　Nae wonder though I should dee !

" For I was ance an Earl's daughter,
    Of noble birth and fame;
And now I'm the mither o' seven sons
    Wha ne'er gat christendame."

He's ta'en his mither by the hand,
    His six brithers also,
And they are on through Elmond-wood
    As fast as they could go.

They wistna weel wha they were gaen,
    And weary were their feet;
They wistna weel wha they were gaen,
    Till they stopped at her father's gate.

" I hae nae money in my pocket,
    But jewel-rings I hae three;
I'll gie them to you, my little son,
    And ye'll enter there for me.

" Ye'll gie the first to the proud porter,
    And he will lat you in;
Ye'll gie the next to the butler-boy,
    And he will show you ben.

" Ye'll gie the third to the minstrel
    That's harping in the ha',
And he'll play gude luck to the bonny boy
    That comes frae the greenwood shaw."

He gied the first to the proud porter,
    And he opened and lat him in;
He gied the next to the butler-boy,
    And he has shown him ben;

He gied the third to the minstrel
    Was harping in the ha',
And he played gude luck to the bonny boy
    That cam' frae the greenwood shaw.

Now when he cam' before the Earl,
    He louted on his knee;
The Earl he turned him round about,
    And the saut tear blint his e'e.

" Win up, win up, thou bonny boy,
    Gang frae my companie;
Ye look sae like my dear daughter,
    My heart will burst in three!"

" If I look like your dear daughter,
    A wonder it is nane;
If I look like your dear daughter,
    I am her eldest son."

" O tell me soon, ye little wee boy,
    Where may my Margaret be?"
" She's e'en now standing at your gates,
    And my six brithers her wi'."

" O where are a' my porter-boys
 That I pay meat and fee,
To open my gates baith braid and wide,
 And let her come in to me ? "

When she cam' in before the Earl,
 She fell doun low on her knee :
" Win up, win up, my daughter dear;
 This day ye'se dine wi' me."

" Ae bit I canna eat, father,
 Ae drop I canna drink,
Till I see Etin, my husband dear;
 Sae lang for him I think ! "

" O where are a' my rangers bold
 That I pay meat and fee,
To search the forest far and wide,
 And bring Hynd Etin to me ? "

Out it speaks the little wee boy :
 " Na, na, this maunna be ;
Without ye grant a free pardon,
 I hope ye'll na him see ! "

" O here I grant a free pardon,
 Well sealed wi' my ain han' ;
And mak' ye search for Hynd **Etin,**
 As sune as ever ye can."

They searched the country braid and wide,
   The forest far and near,
And they found him into Elmond-wood,
   Tearing his yellow hair.

" Win up, win up now, Hynd Etin,
   Win up and boun' wi' me;
For we are come frae the castle,
   And the Earl wad fain you see."

" O lat him tak' my head," he says,
   " Or hang me on a tree;
For sin' I've lost my dear lady,
   My life's nae worth to me!"

" Your head will na be touched, Etin,
   Nor sall you hang on tree;
Your lady's in her father's court,
   And all he wants is thee."

When he cam' in before the Earl,
   He louted on his knee:
" Win up, win up now, Hynd Etin;
   This day ye'se dine wi' me."

As they were at their dinner set,
   The boy he asked a boon:
" I wold we were in haly kirk,
   To get our christendoun.

" For we hae lived in gude greenwood
    These twelve lang years and ane;
But a' this time since e'er I mind
    Was never a kirk within."

" Your asking's na sae great, my boy,
    But granted it sall be:
This day to haly kirk sall ye gang,
    And your mither sall gang you wi'."

When she cam' to the haly kirk,
    She at the door did stan';
She was sae sunken doun wi' shame,
    She couldna come farther ben.

Then out it spak' the haly priest,
    Wi' a kindly word spak' he:
"Come ben, come ben, my lily-flower,
    And bring your babes to me."

LAMKIN.

It's Lamkin was a mason good
    As ever built wi' stane;
He built Lord Wearie's castle,
    But payment gat he nane.

"O pay me, Lord Wearie,
    Come, pay me my fee:"
"I canna pay you, Lamkin,
    For I maun gang o'er the sea."

"O pay me now, Lord Wearie,
  Come, pay me out o' hand:"
"I canna pay you, Lamkin,
  Unless I sell my land."

"O gin ye winna pay me,
  I here sall mak' a vow,
Before that ye come hame again,
  Ye sall hae cause to rue."

Lord Wearie got a bonny ship,
  To sail the saut sea faem;
Bade his lady weel the castle keep,
  Ay till he should come hame.

But the nourice was a fause limmer
  As e'er hung on a tree;
She laid a plot wi' Lamkin,
  Whan her lord was o'er the sea.

She laid a plot wi' Lamkin,
  When the servants were awa',
Loot him in at a little shot-window,
  And brought him to the ha'.

"O where's a' the men o' this house,
  That ca' me Lamkin?"
"They're at the barn-well thrashing;
  'Twill be lang ere they come in."

" And where's the women o' this house,
    That ca' me Lamkin ? "
" They're at the far well washing ;
    'Twill be lang ere they come in."

" And where's the bairns o' this house,
    That ca' me Lamkin ? "
" They're at the school reading ;
    'Twill be night or they come hame."

" O where's the lady o' this house,
    That ca's me Lamkin ? "
" She's up in her bower sewing,
    But we soon can bring her down."

Then Lamkin's tane a sharp knife,
    That hang down by his gaire,
And he has gi'en the bonny babe
    A deep wound and a sair.

Then Lamkin he rocked,
    And the fause nourice she sang,
Till frae ilka bore o' the cradle
    The red blood out sprang.

Then out it spak' the lady,
    As she stood on the stair :
" What ails my bairn, nourice,
    That he's greeting sae sair ?

"O still my bairn, nourice,
 O still him wi' the pap!"
"He winna still, lady,
 For this nor for that."

"O still my bairn, nourice,
 O still him wi' the wand!"
"He winna still, lady,
 For a' his father's land."

"O still my bairn, nourice,
 O still him wi' the bell!"
"He winna still, lady,
 Till you come down yoursel."

O the firsten step she steppit,
 She steppit on a stane;
But the neisten step she steppit,
 She met him Lamkin.

"O mercy, mercy, Lamkin,
 Hae mercy upon me!
Though you've ta'en my young son's life,
 Ye may let mysel be."

"O sall I kill her, nourice,
 Or sall I lat her be?"
"O kill her, kill her, Lamkin,
 For she ne'er was good to me."

"O scour the bason, nourice,
　　And mak' it fair and clean,
For to keep this lady's heart's blood,
　　For she's come o' noble kin."

"There need nae bason, Lamkin,
　　Lat it run through the floor;
What better is the heart's blood
　　O' the rich than o' the poor?"

But ere three months were at an end,
　　Lord Wearie cam' again;
But dowie, dowie was his heart
　　When first he cam' hame.

"O wha's blood is this," he says,
　　"That lies in the chamer?"
"It is your lady's heart's blood;
　　'Tis as clear as the lamer."

"And wha's blood is this," he says,
　　"That lies in my ha'?"
"It is your young son's heart's blood;
　　'Tis the clearest ava."

O sweetly sang the black-bird
　　That sat upon the tree;
But sairer grat Lamkin,
　　When he was condemnd to die.

And bonny sang the mavis,
  Out o' the thorny brake;
But sairer grat the nourice,
  When she was tied to the stake.

HUGH OF LINCOLN.

Four and twenty bonny boys
  Were playing at the ba',
And up it stands him sweet Sir Hugh,
  The flower amang them a'.

He kicked the ba' there wi' his foot,
  And keppit it wi' his knee,
Till even in at the Jew's window
  He gart the bonny ba' flee.

"Cast out the ba' to me, fair maid,
  Cast out that ba' o' mine."
"Never a bit," says the Jew's daughter,
  "Till ye come up an' dine.

"Come up, sweet Hugh, come up, dear Hugh,
  Come up and get the ba'."
"I winna come, I mayna come,
  Without my bonny boys a'."

She's ta'en her to the Jew's garden,
  Where the grass grew lang and green,
She's pu'd an apple red and white,
  To wyle the bonny boy in.

She's wyled him in through ae chamber,
  She's wyled him in through twa,
She's wyled him into the third chamber,
  And that was the warst o' a'.

She's tied the little boy, hands and feet,
  She's pierced him wi' a knife,
She's caught his heart's blood in a golden cup,
  And twinn'd him o' his life.

She row'd him in a cake o' lead,
  Bade him lie still and sleep,
She cast him into a deep draw-well,
  Was fifty fathom deep.

When bells were rung, and mass was sung,
  And every bairn went hame,
Then ilka lady had her young son,
  But Lady Helen had nane.

She's row'd her mantle her about,
  And sair, sair 'gan she weep;
And she ran unto the Jew's house,
  When they were all asleep.

"My bonny Sir Hugh, my pretty Sir Hugh,
  I pray thee to me speak!"
"Lady Helen, come to the deep draw-well
  Gin ye your son wad seek."

Lady Helen ran to the deep draw-well,
  And knelt upon her knee:
"My bonny Sir Hugh, an ye be here,
  I pray thee speak to me!"

"The lead is wondrous heavy, mither,
  The well is wondrous deep;
A keen penknife sticks in my heart,
  It is hard for me to speak.

"Gae hame, gae hame, my mither dear,
  Fetch me my winding-sheet;
And at the back o' merry Lincoln,
  It's there we twa sall meet."

Now Lady Helen she's gane hame,
  Made him a winding-sheet;
And at the back o' merry Lincoln,
  The dead corpse did her meet.

And a' the bells o' merry Lincoln
  Without men's hands were rung;
And a' the books o' merry Lincoln
  Were read without men's tongue:
Never was such a burial
  Sin' Adam's days begun.

FAIR ANNIE.

" LEARN to mak' your bed, Annie,
    And learn to lie your lane;
For I am going ayont the sea,
    A braw bride to bring hame.

" Wi' her I'll get baith gowd and gear,
    Wi' thee I ne'er gat nane;
I got thee as a waif woman,
    I'll leave thee as the same.

" But wha will bake my bridal bread,
    And brew my bridal ale,
And wha will welcome my bright bride,
    That I bring owre the dale ? "

" It's I will bake your bridal bread,
    And brew your bridal ale;
And I will welcome your bright bride,
    When she comes owre the dale."

He set his foot into the stirrup,
    His hand upon the mane;
Says, " It will be a year and a day,
    Ere ye see me again."

Fair Annie stood in her bower door,
 And looked out o'er the lan',
And there she saw her ain gude lord
 Leading his bride by the han'.

She's drest her sons i' the scarlet red,
 Hersel i' the dainty green;
And tho' her cheek look'd pale and wan,
 She weel might hae been a queen.

She called upon her eldest son;
 "Look yonder what ye see,
For yonder comes your father dear,
 Your stepmither him wi'.

"Ye're welcome hame, my ain gude lord,
 To your halls but and your bowers;
Ye're welcome hame, my ain gude lord,
 To your castles and your towers;
Sae is your bright bride you beside,
 She's fairer than the flowers!"

"I thank ye, I thank ye, fair maiden,
 That speaks sae courteouslie;
If I be lang about this house,
 Rewarded ye sall be.

"O what'n a maiden's that," she says,
 "That welcomes you and me?
She is sae like my sister Annie,
 Was stown i' the bower frae me."

O she has served the lang tables,
   Wi' the white bread and the wine;
But ay she drank the wan water,
   To keep her colour fine.

And as she gaed by the first table,
   She leugh amang them a';
But ere she reach'd the second table,
   She loot the tears doun fa'.

She's ta'en a napkin lang and white,
   And hung it on a pin;
And it was a' to dry her e'en,
   As she ga'ed out and in.

When bells were rung, and mass was sung,
   And a' men boun to bed,
The bride but and the bonny bridegroom,
   In ae chamber were laid.

She's ta'en her harp intill her hand,
   To harp this twa asleep;
And ay as she harped and as she sang,
   Full sairly did she weep.

"O seven full fair sons hae I born,
   To the gude lord o' this place;
And O that they were seven young hares,
   And them to rin a race,
And I mysel a gude greyhound,
   And I wad gie them chase!

"O seven full fair sons hae I born
　　To the gude lord o' this ha';
And O that they were seven rattons
　　To rin frae wa' to wa',
And I mysel a gude grey cat,
　　And I wad worry them a'!"

"My goun is on," said the new-come bride,
　　"My shoon are on my feet;
And I will to fair Annie's chamber,
　　And see what gars her greet.

"O wha was't was your father, Annie,
　　And wha was't was your mither?
And had ye ony sister, Annie,
　　Or had ye ony brither?"

"The Earl o' Richmond was my father,
　　His lady was my mither,
And a' the bairns beside mysel,
　　Was a sister and a brither."

"O weel befa' your sang, Annie,
　　I wat ye hae sung in time;
Gin the Earl o' Richmond was your father,
　　I wat sae was he mine.

"O keep your lord, my sister dear,
　　Ye never were wranged by me;
I had but ae kiss o' his merry mouth,
　　As we cam' owre the sea.

There were five ships o' gude red gold
    Cam' owre the seas wi' me,
It's twa o' them will tak' me hame,
    And three I'll leave wi' thee."

THE LAIRD O' DRUM.

The Laird o' Drum is a-hunting gane,
    All in a morning early,
And he has spied a weel-faur'd May,
    A-shearing at her barley.

" My bonny May, my weel-faur'd May,
    O will ye fancy me, O ?
Wilt gae and be the Leddy o' Drum,
    And let your shearing a-be, O ? "

" It's I winna fancy you, kind sir,
    Nor let my shearing a-be, O ;
For I'm ower low to be Leddy Drum,
    And your light love I'll never be, O."

" Gin ye'll cast aff that goun o' gray,
    Put on the silk for me, O,
I'll mak' a vow, and keep it true,
    A light love you'll never be, O."

" My father he is a shepherd mean,
    Keeps sheep on yonder hill, O,
  And ye may gae and speer at him,
    For I am at his will, O."

  Drum is to her father gane,
    Keeping his sheep on yon hill, O:
" I am come to marry your ae daughter,
    If ye'll gie me your good-will, O."

" My dochter can naether read nor write,
    She ne'er was brocht up at scheel, O;
  But weel can she milk baith cow and ewe,
    And mak' a kebbuck weel, O.

" She'll shake your barn, and win your corn,
    And gang to kiln and mill, O;
  She'll saddle your steed in time o' need,
    And draw aff your boots hersell, O."

" I'll learn your lassie to read and write,
    And I'll put her to the scheel, O;
  She shall neither need to saddle my steed,
    Nor draw aff my boots hersell, O.

" But wha will bake my bridal bread,
    Or brew my bridal ale, O;
  And wha will welcome my bonnie bride
    Is mair than I can tell, O."

Four-and-twenty gentlemen
   Gaed in at the yetts of Drum, O:
But no a man has lifted his hat,
   When the Leddy o' Drum cam' in, O.

" Peggy Coutts is a very bonny bride,
   And Drum is big and gawsy ;
But he might hae chosen a higher match
   Than ony shepherd's lassie ! "

Then up bespak his brither John,
   Says, " Ye've done us meikle wrang, O ;
Ye've married ane far below our degree,
   A mock to a' our kin, O."

" Now haud your tongue, my brither John ;
   What needs it thee offend, O ?
I've married a wife to work and win,
   And ye've married ane to spend, O.

" The first time that I married a wife,
   She was far abune my degree, O ;
She wadna hae walked thro' the yetts o' Drum,
   But the pearlin' abune her bree, O,
And I durstna gang in the room where she was,
   But my hat below my knee, O ! "

He has ta'en her by the milk-white hand,
   And led her in himsell, O ;
And in through ha's and in through bowers, —
   " And ye're welcome, Leddy Drum, O."

When they had eaten and well drunken,
    And a' men boun for bed, O,
The Laird of Drum and his Leddy fair,
    In ae bed they were laid, O.

"Gin ye had been o' high renown,
    As ye're o' low degree, O,
We might hae baith gane doun the street
    Amang gude companie, O."

"I tauld ye weel ere we were wed,
    Ye were far abune my degree, O;
But now I'm married, in your bed laid,
    And just as gude as ye, O.

"For an I were dead, and ye were dead,
    And baith in ae grave had lain, O;
Ere seven years were come and gane,
    They'd no ken your dust frae mine, O."

LIZIE LINDSAY.

"WILL ye gae to the Hielands, Lizie Lindsay,
    Will ye gae to the Hielands wi' me?
Will ye gae to the Hielands, Lizie Lindsay,
    And dine on fresh curds and green whey?"

Then out it spak' Lizie's mither,
    An' a gude auld leddy was she:
"Gin ye say sic a word to my daughter,
    I'll gar ye be hangit hie!"

"Keep weel your daughter for me, madam ;
    Keep weel your daughter for me.
I care as leetle for your daughter
    As ye can care for me ! "

Then out spak' Lizie's ain maiden,
    An' a bonnie young lassie was she ;
"Now gin I were heir to a kingdom,
    Awa' wi' young Donald I'd be."

"O say ye sae to me, Nelly ?
    And does my Nelly say sae ?
Maun I leave my father and mither,
    Awa' wi' young Donald to gae ? "

And Lizie's ta'en till her her stockings,
    And Lizie's taen till her her shoon,
And kilted up her green claithing,
    And awa' wi' young Donald she's gane.

The road it was lang and was weary ;
    The braes they were ill for to climb ;
Bonnie Lizie was weary wi' travelling,
    A fit further couldna she win.

"O are we near hame yet, dear Donald ?
    O are we near hame yet, I pray ? "
"We're naething near hame, bonnie Lizie,
    Nor yet the half o' the way."

Sair, O sair was she sighing,
   And the saut tear blindit her e'e :
"Gin this be the pleasures o' luving,
   They never will do wi' me !"

"Now haud your tongue, bonnie Lizie ;
   Ye never sall rue for me ;
Gie me but your luve for my ain luve,
   It is a' that your tocher will be.

"O haud your tongue, bonnie Lizie,
   Altho' that the gait seem lang ;
And you's hae the wale o' gude living
   When to Kincaussie we gang.

"My father he is an auld shepherd,
   My mither she is an auld dey ;
And we'll sleep on a bed o' green rashes,
   And dine on fresh curds and green whey."

They cam' to a hamely puir cottage ;
   The auld woman 'gan for to say :
"O ye're welcome hame, Sir Donald,
   It's yoursell has been lang away."

"Ye mustna ca' me Sir Donald,
   But ca' me young Donald your son ;
For I hae a bonnie young leddy
   Behind me, that's coming alang.

"Come in, come in, bonnie Lizie,
 Come hither, come hither," said he ;
"Altho' that our cottage be leetle,
 I hope we'll the better agree.

"O mak' us a supper, dear mither,
 And mak' it o' curds and green whey ;
And mak' us a bed o' green rashes,
 And cover it o'er wi' fresh hay."

She's made them a bed o' green rashes,
 And covered it o'er wi' fresh hay.
Bonnie Lizie was weary wi' travelling,
 And lay till 'twas lang o' the day.

"The sun looks in o'er the hill-head,
 An' the laverock is liltin' sae gay ;
Get up, get up, bonnie Lizie,
 Ye've lain till it's lang o' the day.

"Ye might hae been out at the shealin',
 Instead o' sae lang to lie ;
And up and helping my mither
 To milk her gaits and her kye."

Then sadly spak' out Lizie Lindsay,
 She spak' it wi' mony a sigh :
"The leddies o' Edinbro' city
 They milk neither gaits nor kye."

"Rise up, rise up, bonnie Lizie,
　　Rise up and mak' yoursel' fine ;
For we maun be at Kincaussie,
　　Before that the clock strikes nine."

But when they cam' to Kincaussie,
　　The porter he loudly doth say,
"O ye're welcome hame, Sir Donald ;
　　It's yoursell has been lang away !"

It's doun then cam' his auld mither,
　　Wi' a' the keys in her han' ;
Saying, "Tak' ye these, bonnie Lizie,
　　For a' is at your comman'."

KATHARINE JANFARIE.

THERE was a may, and a weel-faur'd may,
　　Lived high up in yon glen :
Her name was Katharine Janfarie,
　　She was courted by mony men.

Doun cam' the Laird o' Lamington,
　　Doun frae the South Countrie ;
And he is for this bonny lass,
　　Her bridegroom for to be.

He asked na her father, he asked na her mither,
   He asked na ane o' her kin ;
But he whispered the bonny lassie hersel',
   And did her favor win.

Doun cam' an English gentleman,
   Doun frae the English border ;
And he is for this bonnie lass,
   To keep his house in order.

He asked her father, he asked her mither,
   And a' the lave o' her kin ;
But he never asked the lassie hersel'
   Till on her wedding-e'en.

But she has wrote a lang letter,
   And sealed it wi' her han' ;
And sent it away to Lamington,
   To gar him understan'.

The first line o' the letter he read,
   He was baith fain and glad ;
But or he has read the letter o'er,
   He's turned baith wan and sad.

Then he has sent a messenger,
   To rin through a' his land ;
And four and twenty armèd men
   Were sune at his command.

But he has left his merry men all,
   Left them on the lee;
And he's awa' to the wedding-house,
   To see what he could see.

They all rase up to honor him,
   For he was of high renown;
They all rase up to welcome him,
   And bade him to sit down.

O meikle was the gude red wine
   In silver cups did flow;
But aye she drank to Lamington,
   And fain with him wad go.

"O come ye here to fight, young lord?
   Or come ye here to play?
Or come ye here to drink gude wine
   Upon the wedding-day?"

"I come na here to fight," he said,
   "I come na here to play;
I'll but lead a dance wi' the bonny bride,
   And mount and go my way."

He's caught her by the milk-white hand,
   And by the grass-green sleeve;
He's mounted her hie behind himsel',
   At her kinsfolk spier'd na leave.

It's up, it's up the Couden bank,
    It's doun the Couden brae ;
And aye they made the trumpet soun ,
    "It's a' fair play ! "

Now a' ye lords and gentlemen
    That be of England born,
Come ye na doun to Scotland thus,
    For fear ye get the scorn !

They'll feed ye up wi' flattering words,
    And play ye foul play ;
They'll dress you frogs instead of fish
    Upon your wedding-day !

GLENLOGIE.

THREESCORE o' nobles rade to the king's ha',
But bonnie Glenlogie's the flower o' them a' ;
Wi' his milk-white steed and his bonny black e'e,
"Glenlogie, dear mither, Glenlogie for me ! "

"O haud your tongue, dochter, ye'll get better than he."
"O say na sae, mither, for that canna be ;
    Though Drumlie is richer, and greater than he,
    Yet if I maun lo'e him, I'll certainly dee.

" Where will I get a bonny boy, to win hose and shoon
   Will gae to Glenlogie, and come again soon ? "
" O here am I, a bonny boy, to win hose and shoon,
   Will gae to Glenlogie, and come again soon."

When he gaed to Glenlogie, 'twas " Wash and go dine,"
   'Twas " Wash ye, my pretty boy, wash and go dine."
" O 'twas ne'er my father's fashion, and it ne'er shall be
     mine,
   To gar a lady's errand wait till I dine.

" But there is, Glenlogie, a letter for thee."
   The first line he read, a low smile ga'e he ;
   The next line he read, the tear blindit his e'e ;
   But the last line he read, he gart the table flee.

" Gar saddle the black horse, gar saddle the brown ;
   Gar saddle the swiftest steed e'er rade frae the town ;
   But lang ere the horse was brought round to the green
   O bonnie Glenlogie was twa mile his lane.

When he cam' to Glenfeldy's door, sma' mirth was
     there ;
   Bonnie Jean's mother was tearing her hair ;
" Ye're welcome, Glenlogie, ye're welcome," said she,
" Ye're welcome, Glenlogie, your Jeanie to see."

Pale and wan was she, when Glenlogie gaed ben,
   But red rosy grew she whene'er he sat down ;
   She turned awa' her head, but the smile was in her e'e
" O binna feared, mither, I'll maybe no dee."

GET UP AND BAR THE DOOR.

It fell about the Martinmas time,
    And a gay time it was than,
That our gudewife had puddings to mak'
    And she boil'd them in the pan.

The wind blew cauld frae east and north,
    And blew intil the floor;
Quoth our gudeman to our gudewife,
    "Get up and bar the door."

"My hand is in my hussyskep,
    Gudeman, as ye may see;
An it shou'dna be barr'd this hunder year,
    It's ne'er be barr'd by me."

They made a paction 'tween them twa,
    They made it firm and sure,
That the first word whaever spak,
    Should rise and bar the door.

Than by there came twa gentlemen,
    At twelve o'clock at night,
Whan they can see na ither house,
    And at the door they light.

"Now whether is this a rich man's house,
    Or whether is it a poor?"
But ne'er a word wad ane o' them speak,
    For barring of the door.

And first they ate the white puddings,
    And syne they ate the black:
Muckle thought the gudewife to hersell,
    Yet ne'er a word she spak.

Then ane unto the ither said,
    "Here, man, tak ye my knife;
Do ye tak aff the auld man's beard,
    And I'll kiss the gudewife."

"But there's na water in the house,
    And what shall we do than?"
"What ails ye at the pudding bree
    That boils into the pan?"

O up then started our gudeman,
    An angry man was he;
"Will ye kiss my wife before my een,
    And scaud me wi' pudding bree?"

O up then started our gudewife,
    Gied three skips on the floor;
"Gudeman, ye've spak the foremost word;
    Get up and bar the door."

THE LAWLANDS O' HOLLAND.

" THE luve that I hae chosen,
    I'll therewith be content;
The saut sea sall be frozen
    Before that I repent.
Repent it sall I never
    Until the day I dee;
But the Lawlands o' Holland
    Hae twinned my luve and me.

" My luve he built a bonny ship,
    And set her to the main,
Wi' twenty-four brave mariners
    To sail her out and hame.
But the weary wind began to rise,
    The sea began to rout,
And my luve and his bonny ship
    Turned withershins about.

" There sall nae mantle cross my back,
    No kaim gae in my hair,
Sall neither coal nor candle-light
    Shine in my bower mair;
Nor sall I choose anither luve
    Until the day I dee,
Sin' the Lawlands o' Holland
    Hae twinned my luve and me."

"Noo haud your tongue, my daughter dear,
　　Be still, and bide content;
　There are mair lads in Galloway;
　　Ye needna sair lament."
"O there is nane in Galloway,
　　There's nane at a' for me.
　I never lo'ed a lad but ane,
　　And he's drowned i' the sea."

THE TWA CORBIES.

As I was walking all alane,
I heard twa corbies making a maen;
The tane into the t'ither did say,
"Whaur shall we gang and dine the day?"

"O doun beside yon auld fail dyke,
I wot there lies a new-slain knight;
Nae living kens that he lies there,
But his hawk, his hound, and his lady fair.

"His hound is to the hunting gane,
His hawk to fetch the wildfowl hame,
His lady's ta'en another mate,
Sae we may mak' our dinner sweet.

"O we'll sit on his white hause bane,
And I'll pyke out his bonny blue e'en,
Wi' ae lock o' his gowden hair,
We'll theek our nest when it blaws bare.

" Mony a ane for him makes maen,
　But nane shall ken whaur he is gane;
　Over his banes when they are bare,
　The wind shall blaw for evermair."

HELEN OF KIRCONNELL.

I wad I were where Helen lies;
Night and day on me she cries;
O that I were where Helen lies
　　On fair Kirconnell lea!

Curst be the heart that thought the thought,
And curst the hand that fired the shot,
When in my arms burd Helen dropt,
　　And died to succor me!

O think na but my heart was sair
When my Love dropt down and spak nae mair!
I laid her down wi' meikle care
　　On fair Kirconnell lea.

As I went down the water-side,
Nane but my foe to be my guide,
Nane but my foe to be my guide,
　　On fair Kirconnell lea;

I lighted down my sword to draw,
I hackéd him in pieces sma',
I hackéd him in pieces sma',
　　For her sake that died for me.

O Helen fair, beyond compare!
I'll make a garland of thy hair
Shall bind my heart for evermair
　　Until the day I dee.

O that I were where Helen lies!
Night and day on me she cries;
Out of my bed she bids me rise,
　　Says, "Haste and come to me!"

O Helen fair! O Helen chaste!
If I were with thee, I were blest,
Where thou lies low and takes thy rest
　　On fair Kirconnell lea.

I wad my grave were growing green,
A winding-sheet drawn ower my een,
And I in Helen's arms lying,
　　On fair Kirconnell lea.

I wad I were where Helen lies;
Night and day on me she cries;
And I am weary of the skies,
　　Since my Love died for me.

WALY WALY.

O WALY waly up the bank,
   And waly waly down the brae,
And waly waly yon burn-side
   Where I and my Love wont to gae!
I leant my back unto an aik,
   I thought it was a trusty tree;
But first it bow'd, and syne it brak,
   Sae my true Love did lichtly me.

O waly waly, but love be bonny
   A little time while it is new;
But when 'tis auld, it waxeth cauld
   And fades awa' like morning dew.
O wherefore should I busk my head?
   Or wherefore should I kame my hair?
For my true Love has me forsook,
   And says he'll never loe me mair.

Now Arthur-seat sall be my bed;
   The sheets sall ne'er be prest by me:
Saint Anton's well sall be my drink,
   Since my true Love has forsaken me.
Marti'mas wind, when wilt thou blaw,
   And shake the green leaves aff the tree?
O gentle Death, when wilt thou come?
   For of my life I am wearie.

'Tis not the frost, that freezes fell,
    Nor blawing snaw's inclemencie;
'Tis not sic cauld that makes me cry,
    But my Love's heart grown cauld to me.
When we came in by Glasgow town
    We were a comely sight to see;
My Love was clad in black velvét,
    And I mysell in cramasie.

But had I wist, before I kist,
    That love had been sae ill to win;
I had lockt my heart in a case of gowd
    And pinn'd it with a siller pin.
And, O! that my young babe were born,
    And set upon the nurse's knee,
And I mysell were dead and gane,
    And the green grass growing over me!

LORD RONALD.

"O where hae ye been, Lord Ronald, my son,
    O where hae ye been, my handsome young man?"
"I hae been to the wild wood; mother, make my bed soon,
    For I'm weary wi' hunting, and fain wald lie down."

"Where gat ye your dinner, Lord Ronald, my son?
    Where gat ye your dinner, my handsome young man?"
"I dined wi' my true-love; mother, make my bed soon,
    For I'm weary wi' hunting, and fain wald lie down."

" What gat ye to your dinner, Lord Ronald, my son ?
    What gat ye to your dinner, my handsome young
        man ? "
" I gat eels boil'd in broo'; mother, make my bed soon,
    For I'm weary wi' hunting, and fain wald lie down."

" What became of your bloodhounds, Lord Ronald, my
        son?
    What became of your bloodhounds, my handsome
        young man ? "
" O they swell'd and they died; mother, make my bed
        soon,
    For I'm weary wi' hunting, and fain wald lie down."

" O I fear ye are poison'd, Lord Ronald, my son !
    O I fear ye are poison'd, my handsome young man ! "
" O yes ! I am poison'd ! mother, make my bed soon,
    For I'm sick at the heart, and I fain wald lie down."

EDWARD, EDWARD.

'WHY dois your brand sae drap wi bluid,
        Edward, Edward ?
    Why dois your brand sae drap wi bluid,
        And why sae sad gang yee O ?'
'O I hae killed my hauke sae guid,
        Mither, mither,
    O I hae killed my hauke sae guid,
        And I had nae mair bot hee O.'

'Your haukis bluid was nevir sae reid,
  Edward, Edward,
 Your haukis bluid was nevir sae reid,
  My deir son, I tell thee O.'
'O I hae killed my reid-roan steid,
  Mither, mither,
 O I hae killed my reid-roan steid,
  That erst was sae fair and frie O.'

'Your steid was auld, and ye hae gat mair,
  Edward, Edward,
 Your steid was auld, and ye hae gat mair,
  Sum other dule ye drie O.'
'O I hae killed my fadir deir,
  Mither, mither,
 O I hae killed my fadir deir,
  Alas, and wae is mee O!'

'And whatten penance wul ye drie for that,
  Edward, Edward?
'And whatten penance wul ye drie for that?
  My deir son, now tell me O.'
'Ile set my feit in yonder boat,
  Mither, mither,
 Ile set my feit in yonder boat,
  And Ile fare ovir the sea O.'

'And what wul ye doe wi your towirs and your ha,
  Edward, Edward?
 And what wul ye doe wi your towirs and your ha,
  That were sae fair to see O?'

'Ile let thame stand tul they doun fa,
　　　Mither, mither,
　Ile let thame stand tul they doun fa,
　　For here nevir mair maun I bee O.'

'And what wul ye leive to your bairns and your wife,
　　　Edward, Edward ?
　And what wul ye leive to your bairns and your wife,
　　When ye gang ovir the sea O ? '
'The warldis room, late them beg thrae life,
　　　Mither, mither,
　The warldis room, late them beg thrae life,
　　For thame nevir mair wul I see O.'

'And what wul ye leive to your ain mither deir,
　　　Edward, Edward ?
　And what wul ye leive to your ain mither deir,
　　My deir son, now tell me O.'
'The curse of hell frae me sall ye beir,
　　　Mither, mither,
　The curse of hell frae me sall ye beir,
　　Sic counseils ye gave to me O.'

NOTES.

PAGE 3. **The Wee Wee Man.** Mainly after Herd. Given also by Motherwell, Buchan, and Kinloch, and in Caw's "Poetical Museum." *Shathmont*, a six inch measure. *Lap*, leaped. *Jimp*, neat.

P. 4. **Tamlane.** Mainly after Aytoun's collated version. Stanzas 16–19, obtained by Scott "from a gentleman residing near Langholm," are too modern in diction to harmonize well with the rest, but are retained here because of their fidelity to the ancient beliefs of the country folk about fairies. Widely varying versions are given in Johnson's "Museum," communicated by Burns, under title of *Tam Lin*; in the Glenriddell MS. under title of *Young Tom Line*; by Herd, under title of *Kertonha*, corruption of Carterhaugh; by Motherwell, under titles of *Young Tamlin* and *Tomaline*; by Buchan, under titles of *Tam-a-line* and *Tam a-Lin*; and in the Campbell MS. under title of *Young Tam Lane*. There are humorous Scottish songs, too, of *Tam o Lin*, *Tam o the Linn*, *Tom a Lin*, and *Tommy Linn*. The ballad is of respectable antiquity, the *Tayl of the Yong Tamlene* and the dance of *Thom of Lyn* being noticed in a work as old as the "Complaynt of Scotland" (1548); yet it seems to have no Continental cousins, but to be strictly of Scottish origin. It belongs to Selkirkshire, whose peasants still point out upon the plain of Carterhaugh, about a mile above Selkirk, the fairy rings in the grass. *Preen'd*, decked. *Gars*, makes. *Bree*, brow. *Sained*, baptized. *Snell*, keen. *Teind*, tithe. *Borrow*, ransom. *Cast a compass*, draw a circle. *Elrish*, elvish. *Gin*, if. *Maik*, mate. *Aske*, lizard. *Bale*, fire. *But and*, and also. *Tree*, wood. *Coft*, bought.

P. 12. **True Thomas.** Mainly after Scott. This is one of the ballads written down from the recital of the "good Mrs. Brown," to whose admirable memory ballad-lovers are so deeply indebted. It is given in the Brown MS. as *Thomas Rymer and Queen of Elfland*; in the Campbell MS. as *Thomas the Rhymer.* Scott obtained his excellent version from " a lady residing not far from Ercildoune." This Thomas the Rhymer, or True Thomas, or Thomas of Ercildoune, was a veritable personage, who dwelt in the village of Ercildoune situate by " Leader's silver tide " some two miles above its junction with the Tweed. Tradition has it that his date was the thirteenth century and his full name Thomas Learmont. He was celebrated as poet and prophet, the rustics believing that his gift of soothsaying was imparted by the Fairy Queen, who kept him with her in Elfland for seven years, permitting him then to return to the upper world for a season and utter his oracles, but presently recalling him to her mysterious court. A fragmentary old poem, showing probable traces, as Jamieson suggests, of the Rhymer's own authorship, tells this famous adventure in language whose antiquated form cannot disguise its sweetness. The melancholy likelihood seems to be that True Thomas was a fibbing Thomas, after all, and invented this story of his sojourn in Elfland to gain credit for his poetical prophecies, which claim to have first proceeded from the mouth of the Fairy Queen, when

> " Scho broghte h᷊m agayne to Eldone tree,
>   Vndir nethe that grenewode spr␣ye ;
> In Huntlee bannkes es mery to bee,
>   Whare fowles synges bothe nyght and daye."

Ferlie, wonder. *Ilka tett,* each lock (of hair). *Louted,* bowed. *Harp and carp,* play and talk. *Leven,* lawn. *Stern-light,* star-light. *Dought,* could.

PAGE 15. **The Elfin Knight.** After Aytoun's version framed by collation from copies given by Motherwell, Kinloch, and Buchan. These were in the main recovered by recitation, although there is a broadside copy of the ballad in the Pepysian collection at Cambridge. Fragments of the story have been handed down in tavern-songs and nursery-rhymes, and it is to be found, more or less disguised, in the literatures of many countries, European and Asiatic. It is only in our own versions, however, that the outwitted knight is a supernatural being, usually an elf, though sometimes degenerating into " the Deil." Nowhere out of canny Scotland does his ungallantry debar him from the human ranks. *Sark,* shirt. *Gin,* if. *Tyne,* prong. *Shear,* reap. *Bigg,* build. *Loof,* hollow of the hand. *But* (candle, etc.), without (candle, etc.)

PAGE 18. **Lady Isobel and the Elf-Knight**. Mainly after Buchan's version entitled *The Water o' Wearie's Well*, although it is in another version given by Buchan, under title of *The Gowans sae Gay*, that the name of the lady is disclosed, and the elfin nature of the eccentric lover revealed. In that ballad Lady Isobel falls in love with the elf-knight on hearing him

> " blawing his horn,
> The first morning in May,"

and this more tuneful version retains in the first two stanzas a fading trace of the fairy element and the magic music, the bird, whose song may be supposed to have caused the lady's heart-ache, being possibly the harper in elfin disguise. In most of the versions, however, the knight is merely a human knave, usually designated as Fause Sir John, and the lady is frequently introduced as May Colven or Colvin or Collin or Collean, though also as Pretty Polly. The story is widely circulated, appearing in the folk-songs of nearly all the nations of northern and southern Europe. It has been suggested that the popular legend may be " a wild shoot from the story of Judith and Holofernes." *Dowie*, doleful.

P. 21. **Tom Thumbe**. After Ritson, with omissions. Ritson prints from a manuscript dated 1630, the oldest copy known to be extant, but the story itself can be traced much further back and was evidently a prime favorite with the English rustics. The plain, often doggerel verse, and the rough, often coarse humor of this ballad make it appear at striking disadvantage among the Scottish folk-songs, essentially poetic as even the rudest of them are. Tom Thumbe, it must be confessed, is but a clumsy sort of elf, and the ballad as a whole can hardly be said to have a fairy atmosphere. Yet it is of value as adding to the data for a comparison between the English and the Scottish peasantry, as throwing light on the fun-loving spirit, the sports and practical joking of Merrie England, as showing the tenacity of the Arthurian tradition, together with the confusion of chivalric memories, as displaying the ignorant credulity of the popular mind toward science no less than toward history, and as illustrating, by giving us in all this bald, sing-song run of verses, here and there a sweet or dainty fancy and at least one stanza of exquisite tenderness and grace, the significant fact that in the genuine old English ballads beauty is not the rule, but the surprise. *Counters*, coin-shaped pieces of metal, ivory, or wood, used in reckoning. *Points,* here probably the bits of tin plate used to tag the strands of cotton yarn with which, in lieu of buttons, the common folk fastened their garments. The points worn by the nobles were laces or silken strands ornamented with aiglets of gold or silver.

PAGE 33. **Kempion.** After Allingham's version collated from copies given by Scott, Buchan, and Motherwell, with a touch or two from the kindred ballad *The Laidley Worm of Spindleston Heugh.* Buchan and Motherwell make the name of the hero Kemp Owyne. Similar ballads are known in Iceland and Denmark, and the main features of the story appear in both the classic and romantic literatures. *Weird,* destiny. *Dree,* suffer. *Borrowed,* ransomed. *Arblast bow,* cross-bow. *Stythe,* place. *Louted,* bowed.

P. 37. **Alison Gross.** After Jamieson's version taken from the recitation of Mrs. Brown. Child claims that this tale is a variety of *Beauty and the Beast. Lemman,* lover. *Gar,* make. *Toddle,* twine. *Seely Court,* Happy Court or Fairy Court. See English Dictionary for changes of meaning in *silly.*

P. 39. **The Wife of Usher's Well.** After Scott, with a stanza or two from Chambers, both versions being recovered by recitation. Although this is scarcely more than a fragment, it is well-nigh unsurpassed for genuine ballad beauty, the mere touches of narrative suggesting far deeper things than they actually relate. *Martinmas,* the eleventh of November. *Carline wife,* old peasant-woman. *Fashes,* troubles. *Birk,* birch. *Syke,* marsh. *Sheugh,* trench. *Channerin',* fretting. *Gin,* if. *Byre,* cow-house.

P. 41. **A Lyke-Wake Dirge.** After Scott. This dirge belongs to the north of England and is said to have been chanted, in Yorkshire, over the dead, down to about 1624. *Lyke-Wake,* dead-watch. *Sleete,* salt, it being the old peasant custom to place a quantity of this on the breast of the dead. *Whinny-muir,* Furze-moor. A manuscript found by Ritson in the Cotton Library states: " When any dieth, certaine women sing a song to the dead bodie, recyting the journey that the partye deceased must goe; and they are of beliefe (such is their fondnesse) that once in their lives, it is good to give a pair of new shoes to a poor man, for as much as, after this life, they are to pass barefoote through a great launde, full of thornes and furzen, except by the meryte of the almes aforesaid they have redemed the forfeyte; for, at the edge of the launde, an oulde man shall meet them with the same shoes that were given by the partie when he was lyving; and, after he hath shodde them, dismisseth them to go through thick and thin, without scratch or scalle." *Brigg o' Dread*, Bridge of Dread. Descriptions of this Bridge of Dread are found in various Scottish poems, the most minute being given in the legend of *Sir Owain*. Compare the belief of the Mahometan that in his approach to the judgment-seat, he must traverse a bar of red-hot iron, stretched across a bottomless abyss, true believers being upheld by their good works, while the wicked fall headlong into the gulf.

Page 43. **Proud Lady Margaret.** After Aytoun. The original versions of this ballad, as given by Scott, Buchan, Dixon, and Laing, differ widely. It is known under various titles, *The Courteous Knight*, *The Jolly Hind Squire*, *The Knicht o Archerdale*, *Fair Margret*, and *Jolly Janet*. Similar ballads are rife in France, although in these it is more frequently the ghost of a dead lady who admonishes her living lover. *Wale*, choose. *Ill-washen feet*, etc., in allusion to the custom of washing and dressing the dead for burial. *Feckless*, worthless. *Pirie's chair* remains an unsolved riddle of the ballad, editors and commentators not being as good at guessing as the ghost.

P. 48. **The Twa Sisters o' Binnorie.** Mainly after Aytoun. There are many versions of this ballad in Scotland, England, Wales and Ireland, varying widely in titles, refrains, and indeed in everything save the main events of the story. A broadside copy appeared as early as 1656. Ballads on the same subject are very popular among the Scandinavian peoples, and traces of the story are found as far away as China and South Africa. *Twined*, parted. *Make*, mate. *Gar'd*, made. Although Lockhart would have the burden pronounced Binnŏrie, a more musical effect is secured by following Jamieson and pronouncing Binnōrie.

P. 53. **The Demon Lover.** After Scott. Buchan has a version under title of *James Herries*, the demon being here transformed into a lover who has died abroad and comes in spirit guise to punish his " Jeanie Douglas " for her broken vows. Motherwell gives a graphic fragment. *Ilka*, every. *Drumly*, dark. *Won*, dwell.

P. 56. **Riddles Wisely Expounded.** Mainly after Motherwell. There are several broadsides, differing slightly, of this ballad. Riddling folk-songs similar to this in general features have been found among the Germans and Russians and in Gaelic literature. *Speird,* asked. *Unco*, uncanny. *Gin*, if. *Pies*, magpies. *Clootie*, see Burns's *Address to the Deil.*

> " O thou! whatever title suit thee,
> Auld Hornie, Satan, Nick, or Clootie," etc.

PAGE 61. **Sir Patrick Spens.** After Scott. There are many versions of

> " The grand old ballad of Sir Patrick Spence,"

as Coleridge so justly terms it, the fragment in the *Reliques* being unsurpassed among them all for poetic beauty. Herd's longer copy, like several of the others, runs song-fashion:

> " They had not saild upon the sea
> A league but merely nine, O,
> When wind and weit and snaw and sleit
> Cam' blawin' them behin', O."

Motherwell gives the ballad in four forms, in one of them the skipper being dubbed Sir Patrick, in another Earl Patrick, in another Young Patrick, and in yet another Sir Andrew Wood. Jamieson's version puts into Sir Patrick's mouth an exclamation that reflects little credit upon his sailor character:

> " O wha is this, or wha is that,
> Has tald the king o' me ?
> For I was never a gude seaman,
> Nor ever intend to be."

But with a few such trifling exceptions, the tone toward the skipper is universally one of earnest respect and sympathy, the keynote of every ballad being the frank, unconscious heroism of this " gude Sir Patrick Spens." In regard to the foundation for the story, Scott maintains that "the king's daughter of Noroway" was Margaret, known to history as the Maid of Norway, daughter of Eric, king of Norway, and of Margaret, daughter of Alexander III. of Scotland. This last-named monarch died in 1285, the Maid of Norway, his yellow-haired little granddaughter, being the heiress to his crown. The Maid of Norway died, however, before she was of age to assume control of her turbulent Scottish kingdom. Scott surmises, on the authority of the ballad, that Alexander, desiring to have the little princess reared in the country she was to rule, sent this expedition for her during his life-time. No record of such a voyage is extant, although possibly the presence of the king is a bold example of poetic license, and the reference is to an earlier and more disastrous embassy than that finally sent by the Regency of Scotland, after Alexander's death, to their young queen, Sir Michael Scott of wizard fame being at that time one of the ambassadors. Finlay, on the other hand, places this ballad in the days of James III., who married Margaret of Denmark. Here we have historic testimony of the voyage, but none of the shipwreck, — yet against any one of these theories the natural objection is brought that so lamentable a disaster, involving so many nobles of the realm, would hardly be suffered to escape the pen of the chronicler. Motherwell, Maidment, and Aytoun, relying on a corroborative passage in Fordun's *Scotichronicon*, hold with good appearance of reason that the ballad pictures what is known as an actual shipwreck, on the return from Norway of those Scottish lords who had escorted thither the bride of Eric, the elder Margaret, afterward mother of the little Maid of Norway. The ballad itself well bears out this theory, especially in the taunt flung at the Scottish gallants for lingering too long in nuptial festivities on the inhospitable Norwegian coast. The date of this marriage was 1281. *Skeely*, skilful. *Gane*, sufficed. *Half-fou*, half-bushel. *Gurly*, stormy.

PAGE 65. **The Battle of Otterburne.** After Scott. There are several Scottish versions of this spirit-stirring ballad, and also an English version, first printed in the fourth edition of the *Reliques.* The English ballad, naturally enough, dwells more on the prowess of Percy and his countrymen in the combat than on their final discomfiture. A vivid account of the battle of Otterburne may be found in Froissart's *Chronicles.* In brief, it was a terrible slaughter brought about by the eager pride and ambition of those two hot-blooded young chieftains, James, Earl of Douglas, and the redoubtable Harry Percy. Yet the generosity of the leaders and the devoted loyalty of their men throw a moral splendor over the scene of bloodshed. In the year 1388 Douglas, at the head of three thousand Scottish spears, made a raid into Northumberland and, before the walls of Newcastle, engaged Percy in single combat, capturing his lance with the attached pennon. Douglas retired in triumph, brandishing his trophy, but Hotspur, burning with shame, hurriedly mustered the full force of the Marches and, following hard upon the Scottish rear, made a night attack upon the camp of Douglas at Otterburne, about twenty miles from the frontier. Then ensued a moonlight battle, gallant and desperate, fought on either side with unflinching bravery, and ending in the defeat of the English, Percy being taken prisoner. But the Scots bought their glory dear by the loss of their noble leader, who, when the English troops, superior in number, were gaining ground, dashed forward with impetuous courage, cheering on his men, and cleared a way with his swinging battle-axe into the heart of the enemy's ranks. Struck down by three mortal wounds, he died in the midst of the fray, urging with his failing breath these last requests upon the little guard of kinsmen who pressed about him: "First, that yee keep my death close both from our owne folke and from the enemy; then, that ye suffer not my standard to be lost or cast downe; and last, that ye avenge my death, and bury me at Melrosse with my father. If I could hope for these things," he added, "I should die with the greater contentment; for long since I heard a prophesie that a dead man should winne a field, and I hope in God it shall be I." *Lammas-tide,* the first of August. *Muirmen,* moormen. *Harried,* plundered. *The tane,* the one. *Fell,* skin. (The inference is that Percy was rescued by his men.) *Gin,* if. *Burn,* brook. *Kale,* broth. *Fend,* sustain. *Bent,* open field. *Pallions,* tents (pavilions). *Branking,* prancing. *Wargangs,* wagons. *Ayont,* beyond. *Hewmont,* helmet. *Swakkit,* smote. *Bracken,* fern.

PAGE 71. **The Hunting of the Cheviot.** After Hearne, who first printed it from a manuscript in the Ashmolean collection at Oxford. It was next printed in the *Reliques,* under title of *Chevy-Chase,* — a title now reserved for the later and inferior broadside version which was singularly popular throughout the seventeenth century and is still better known than this far more spirited original. "With regard to the subject of this ballad," — to quote from Bishop Percy, — "although it has no countenance from history, there is room to think it had originally some foundation in fact. It was one of the laws of the Marches, frequently renewed between the nations, that neither party should hunt in the other's borders, without leave from the proprietors or their deputies. There had long been a rivalship between the two martial families of Percy and Douglas, which, heightened by the national quarrel, must have produced frequent challenges and struggles for superiority, petty invasions of their respective domains, and sharp contests for the point of honour; which would not always be recorded in history. Something of this kind, we may suppose, gave rise to the ancient ballad of the *Hunting o' the Cheviat.* Percy,

Earl of Northumberland, had vowed to hunt for three days in the
Scottish border, without condescending to ask leave from Earl
Douglas, who was either lord of the soil, or lord warden of the
Marches. Douglas would not fail to resent the insult, and endeavour
to repel the intruders by force; this would naturally produce a sharp
conflict between the two parties; something of which, it is probable,
did really happen, though not attended with the tragical circum-
stances recorded in the ballad: for these are evidently borrowed from
the Battle of Otterbourn, a very different event, but which aftertimes
would easily confound with it." The date of the ballad cannot, of
course, be strictly ascertained. It was considered old in the middle
of the sixteenth century, being mentioned in *The Complaynt of Scotland* (1548) among the "sangis of natural music of the antiquite."
Not much can be said for its "natural music," yet despite its rough-
ness of form and enviable inconsistencies of spelling, it has always
found grace with the poets. Rare Ben Jonson used to say that he
would rather have been the author of *Chevy Chase* than of all his
works; Addison honored the broadside version with two critiques in
the *Spectator;* and Sir Philip Sidney, though lamenting that the ballad
should be "so evil apparrelled in the dust and cobwebs of that un-
civill age," breaks out with the ingenuous confession: "I never heard
the olde song of Percy and Duglas that I found not my heart mooved
more then with a trumpet, and yet is it sung but by some blinde
crouder, with no rougher voice then rude stile." *Mauger,* despite.
Let, hinder. *Meany,* company. *Shyars,* shires. *Bomen,* bowmen.
Byckarte, moved quickly, rattling their weapons. *Bent,* open field.
Aras, arrows. *Wyld,* wild creatures, as deer. *Shear,* swiftly. *Grevis,*
groves. *Glent,* glanced, flashed by. *Oware off none,* hour of noon.
Mort, death-signal (as used in hunting.) *Quyrry,* quarry, slaughtered
game. *Bryttlynge,* cutting up. *Wyste,* knew. *Byll and brande,* axe
and sword. *Glede,* live coal. *The ton,* the one. *Yerle,* earl. *Cors,*
curse. *Nam,* name. *Wat,* wot, know. *Sloughe,* slew. *Byddys,*
abides. *Wouche,* injury. *Ost,* host. *Suar,* sure. *Many a doughete
the garde to dy,* many a doughty (knight) they caused to die. *Basnites,* small helmets. *Myneyeple,* maniple (of many folds), a coat worn
under the armor. *Freyke,* warrior. *Swapte,* smote. *Myllàn,* Milàn.
Hight, promise. *Spendyd,* grasped (spanned). *Corsiare,* courser.
Blane, halted. *Dynte,* stroke. *Halyde,* hauled. *Stour,* press of battle. *Dre,* endure. *Hinde,* gentle. *Hewyne in to,* hewn in two. *The*

mayde them byears, they made them biers. *Makys*, mates. *Carpe off care*, tell of sorrow. *March perti*, the Border district. *Lyff-tenant*, lieutenant. *Weal*, clasp. *Brook*, enjoy. *Quyte*, avenged. *That tear begane this spurn*, that wrong caused this retaliation. *Reane*, rain. *Ballys bete*, sorrows amend.

PAGE 83. **Edom o' Gordon.** After Aytoun. This ballad was first printed at Glasgow, 1755, as taken down by Sir David Dalrymple "from the recitation of a lady," and was afterwards inserted — "interpolated and corrupted," says the unappeasable Ritson — in Percy's *Reliques*. Ritson himself published a genuine and ancient copy from a manuscript belonging apparently to the last quarter of the sixteenth century and preserved in the Cotton Library. The ballad is known under two other titles, *Captain Car* and *The Burning o' Loudon Castle*. Notwithstanding this inexactitude in names, the ballad has an historical basis. In 1571 Adam Gordon, deputy-lieutenant of the North of Scotland for Queen Mary, was engaged in a struggle against the clan Forbes, who upheld the Reformed Faith and the King's party. Gordon was successful in two sharp encounters, but "what glory and renown he obtained of these two victories," says the contemporary History of King James the Sixth, "was all cast down by the infamy of his next attempt; for immediately after this last conflict he directed his soldiers to the castle of Towie, desiring the house to be rendered to him in the Queen's name; which was obstinately refused by the lady, and she burst forth with certain injurious words. And the soldiers being impatient, by command of their leader, Captain Ker, fire was put to the house, wherein she and the number of twenty-seven persons were cruelly burnt to the death."

Martinmas, the eleventh of November. *Hauld*, stronghold. *Toun*, enclosed place. *Buskit*, made ready. *Light*, alighted. *But and*, and also. *Dree*, suffer. *But an*, unless. *Wude*, mad. *Dule*, pain. *Reek*, smoke. *Nourice*, nurse. *Jimp*, slender. *Row*, roll. *Tow*, throw. *Busk and boun*, up and away. *Freits*, ill omens. *Lowe*, blaze. *Wichty*, sturdy. *Bent*, field. *Teenfu'*, sorrowful. *Wroken*, avenged.

P. 89. **Kinmont Willie.** After Scott. This dashing ballad appeared for the first time in the *Border Minstrelsy*, having been "preserved by tradition," says Scott, "on the West Borders, but much mangled by reciters, so that some conjectural emendations have been absolutely necessary to render it intelligible." The facts in the case seem to be that in 1596 Salkeld, deputy of Lord Scroope, English

Warden of the West Marches, and Robert Scott, for the Laird of Buccleuch, Keeper of Liddesdale, met on the border line for conference in the interest of the public weal. The truce, that on such occasions extended from the day of the meeting to the next day at sunset, was this time violated by a party of English soldiers, who seized upon William Armstrong of Kinmonth, a notorious freebooter, as he, attended by but three or four men, was returning from the conference, and lodged him in Carlisle Castle. The Laird of Buccleuch, after treating in vain for his release, raised two hundred horse, surprised the castle and carried off the prisoner without further ceremony. This exploit the haughty Queen of England " esteemed a great affront " and " stormed not a little " against the " bauld Buccleuch." *Haribee,* the place of execution at Carlisle. *Liddel-rack,* a ford on the Liddel. *Reiver,* robber. *Hostelrie,* inn. *Lawing,* reckoning. *Garr'd,* made. *Basnet,* helmet. *Curch,* cap. *Lightly,* set light by. *Low,* blaze. *Splent on spauld,* armor on shoulder. *Woodhouselee,* a house belonging to Buccleuch, on the Border. *Herry,* harry, spoil. *Corbie,* crow. *Wons,* dwells. *Lear,* lore. *Row-footed,* rough-footed (?). *Spait,* flood. *Garr'd,* made. *Stear,* stir. *Coulters,* ploughshares. *Forehammers,* the large hammers that strike before the small, sledgehammers. *Fley'd,* frightened. *Spier,* inquire. *Hente,* caught. *Maill,* rent. *Airns,* irons. *Wood,* mad. *Furs,* furrows. *Trew,* trust.

PAGE 97. **King John and the Abbot of Canterbury.** After Percy, who printed from an ancient black-letter copy. There are three other broadside versions of this popular ballad extant, and at least one older version has been lost. Similar riddle-stories are to be found in almost all European literatures. There is nothing in this ballad save the name of King John, with his reputation for unjust and high-handed dealing, that can be called traditional. *Deere,* harm. *Stead,* place. *St. Bittel,* St. Botolph (?).

P. 101. **Robin Hood Rescuing the Widow's Three Sons.** After Ritson, who has collected in two volumes the ballads of Robin Hood. This is believed to be one of the oldest of them all. A concise introduction to the Robin Hood ballads is given by Mr. Hales in the *Percy Folio MS.* vol. i. This legendary king of Sherwood Forest is more rightfully the hero of English song than his splendid rival, the Keltic King Arthur,

> " whose name, a ghost,
> Streams like a cloud, man-shaped, from mountain peak,
> And cleaves to cairn and cromlech still."

Yet there is scarcely less doubt as to the actual existence of a flesh-and-blood Robin Hood than there is as to the actual existence of a flesh-and-blood King Arthur. But let History look to her own; Literature need have no scruple in claiming both the archer-prince of outlaws and the blameless king of the Table Round. Robber chieftain or democratic agitator, romantic invention or Odin-myth, it is certain that by the fourteenth century Robin Hood was a familiar figure in English balladry. We have our first reference to this generous-hearted rogue of the greenwood, who is supposed by Ritson to have lived from 1160 to 1247, in Langlande's *Piers Ploughman* (1362). There are brief notices of the popular bandit in Wyntoun's *Scottish Chronicle* (1420), Fordun's *Scotichronicon* (1450), and Mair's *Historia Majoris Brittaniæ* (1521). Famous literary allusions occur in Latimer's *Sixth Sermon before Edward VI.* (1548), in Drayton's *Polyolbion* (1613), and Fuller's *Worthies of England* (1662). The Robin Hood ballads illustrate to the full the rough and heavy qualities, both of form and thought, that characterize all our English folk-songs as opposed to the Scottish. We feel the difference instantly when a minstrel from over the Border catches up the strain:

> " There's mony ane sings o' grass, o' grass,
>   And mony ane sings o' corn;
>   And mony ane sings o' Robin Hood,
>   Kens little whar' he was born.

> " It was na' in the ha', the ha',
>   Nor in the painted bower;
>   But it was in the gude greenwood,
>   Amang the lily flower."

Yet these rude English ballads have just claims on our regard. They stand our feet squarely upon the basal rock of Saxon ethics, they breathe a spirit of the sturdiest independence, and they draw, in a few strong strokes, so fresh a picture of the joyous, fearless life led under the green shadows of the deer-haunted forest by that memorable band, bold Robin and Little John, Friar Tuck and George a Green, Will Scarlett, Midge the Miller's Son, Maid Marian and the rest, that we gladly succumb to a charm recognized by Shakespeare himself: " They say he is already in the forest of Arden, and a many merry men with him; and there they live like the old Robin Hood of England; they say many young gentlemen flock to him every day, and fleet the time carelessly, as they did in the golden world." — *As You Like It.*

PAGE 106. **Robin Hood and Allin A Dale.** After Ritson. This ballad is first found in broadside copies of the latter half of the seventeenth century. *Lin,* pause.

P. 111. **Robin Hood's Death and Burial.** After Ritson, who made his version from a collation of two copies given in a York garland.

P. 117. **Annie of Lochroyan.** After Aytoun, who improves on Jamieson's version. This beautiful ballad is given in varying forms by Herd, Scott, Buchan, and others. Lochroyan, or Loch Ryan, is a bay on the south-west coast of Scotland. *Jimp,* slender. *Gin,* if. *Greet,* cry. *Tirl'd,* rattled. *But and,* and also. *Warlock,* wizard. *Sinsyne,* since then. *Hooly,* slowly. *Deid,* death. *Syne,* then.

P. 123. **Lord Thomas and Fair Annet.** After Aytoun, who adds to the first twenty-four stanzas of the copy given in the *Reliques* a concluding fourteen taken from Jamieson's *Sweet Willie and Fair Annie.* The unfortunate lady elsewhere figures as *The Nut-Brown Bride* and *Fair Ellinor.* There are Norse ballads which relate something akin to the same story. *Gif,* if. *Rede,* counsel. *Owsen,* oxen. *Billie,* an affectionate term for brother. *Byre,* cow-house. *Fadge,* clumsy woman. *Sheen,* shoes. *Tift,* whiff. *Gin,* if. *Cleiding,* clothing. *Bruik,* enjoy. *Kist,* chest. *Lee,* lonesome. *Till,* to. *Dowie,* doleful. *Sark,* shroud. *But and,* and also. *Birk,* birch.

P. 129. **The Banks o' Yarrow.** After Allingham's collated version. There are many renderings of this ballad, which Scott declares to be a great favorite among the peasantry of the Ettrick forest, who firmly believe it founded on fact. The river Yarrow, so favored of the poets, flows through a valley in Selkirkshire and joins the Tweed above the town of Selkirk. The *Tennies* is a farm below the Yarrow kirk. *Lawing,* reckoning. *Dawing,* dawn. *Marrow,* mate. *Dowie,* doleful. *Leafu',* lawful. *Binna,* be not.

P. 133. **The Douglas Tragedy.** After Scott. This ballad is likewise known under titles of *Earl Brand, Lady Margaret* and *The Child of Ell.* Danish, Swedish, Norwegian and Icelandic ballads relate a kindred story, and the incident of the intertwining plants that spring from the graves of hapless lovers, occurs in the folk-lore of almost all peoples. *Bugelet,* a small bugle. *Dighted,* strove to stanch. *Plat,* intertwined.

PAGE 136. **Fine Flowers i' the Valley.** After Aytoun, his version, though taken down from recitation, being in reality a compound of Herd's and Jamieson's. Aytoun claims that "this is perhaps the most popular of all the Scottish ballads, being commonly recited and sung even at the present day." Different refrains are often employed, and the ballad is frequently given under title of *The Cruel Brother.* Stories similar to this are found in the balladry of both northern and southern Europe. *Marrow,* mate. *Close,* avenue leading from the door to the street. *Louting,* bowing. *Its lane,* alone.

P. 140. **The Gay Goss-Hawk.** Mainly after Motherwell, although his version is entitled *The Jolly Goshawk.* The epithet *Gay* has the sanction of Scott and Jamieson. Buchan gives a rendering of this ballad under title of *The Scottish Squire.* *Whin,* furze. *Bigly,* spacious. *Sark,* shroud. *Claith,* cloth. *Steeking,* stitching. *Gar'd,* made. *Chive,* morsel. *Skaith,* harm.

P. 145. **Young Redin.** After Allingham's collated copy. There are many versions of this ballad, the hero being variously known as Young Hunting, Earl Richard, Lord William, Lord John and Young Redin. *Birl'd,* plied. *Douk,* dive. *Weil-head,* eddy. *Linn,* the pool beneath a cataract. *Brin,* burn. *Balefire,* bonfire.

P. 150. **Willie and May Margaret.** After Allingham's copy framed by collating Jamieson's fragmentary version with Buchan's ballad of *The Drowned Lovers.* *Stour,* wild. *Pot,* a pool in a river. *Dowie den,* doleful hollow. *Tirled,* rattled. *Steeked,* fastened. *Brae,* hillside. *Sowm,* swim. *Minnie,* affectionate term for mother.

P. 155. **Young Beichan.** Mainly after Jamieson, his version being based upon a copy taken down from the recitation of the indefatigable Mrs. Brown and collated with a manuscript and stall copy, both from Scotland, a recited copy from the North of England, and a short version "picked off an old wall in Piccadilly." Of this ballad of *Young Beichan* there are numerous renderings, the name of the hero undergoing many variations, — Bicham, Brechin, Beachen, Bekie, Bateman, Bondwell — and the heroine, although Susie Pye or Susan Pye in ten of the fourteen versions, figuring also as Isbel, Essels, and Sophia. It was probably an English ballad at the start, but bears the traces of the Scottish minstrels who were doubtless prompt to borrow it. There is likelihood enough that the ballad was originally suggested by the legend of Gilbert Becket, father of the great archbishop; the story running that Becket, while a captive in Holy Land, plighted his troth to the daughter of a Saracenic prince. When the crusader had made good his escape, the lady followed him, inquiring her way to "England" and to "London," where she wandered up and down the streets, constantly repeating her lover's name, "Gilbert," the third and last word of English that she knew, until finally she found him, and all her woes were put to flight by the peal of wedding bells. *Termagant*, the name given in the old romances to the God of the Saracens. *Pine*, pain. *Sheave*, slice. *But and*, and also. *Dreed*, endured.

PAGE 162. **Gilderoy.** After the current version adapted from the original by Sir Alexander Halket or his sister, Lady Elizabeth Wardlaw, the composer of *Hardyknute*. There is extant a black-letter broadside printed in England as early as 1650, and the ballad appears in several miscellanies of later date. The reviser added the sixth, seventh, and eighth stanzas. It is mortifying to learn that this "winsome Gilderoy"—the name, properly Gillie roy, signifying in Gaelic "the red-haired lad"—was in reality one Patrick Mac-Gregor, who was hanged at the cross of Edinburgh, 1638, as a common cateran or free-booter. That the romantic element in the ballad so outweighs the historical, must account for its classification here. *Soy*, silk. *Cess*, black-mail. *Gear*, property.

P. 166. **Bonny Barbara Allan.** After the version given in Ramsay's *Tea-Table Miscellany* and followed by Herd, Ritson, and others. Percy prints with this in the *Reliques* a longer, but poorer copy. In Pepys's *Diary*, Jan. 2, 1666, occurs an allusion to the "little Scotch song of Barbary Allen." *Gin*, if. *Hooly*, slowly. *Jow*, knell.

P. 168. **The Gardener.** After Kinloch. Buchan gives a longer, but less valuable version. *Jimp*, slender. *Weed*, dress. *Camorine*, camomile. *Kail-blade*, cabbage-leaf. *Cute*, ankle. *Brawn*, calf. *Blaewort*, witch bells.

P. 169. **Etin the Forester.** Collated. No single version of this ballad is satisfactory, not Kinloch's fine fragment, *Hynde Etin*, nor Buchan's complete but inferior version, *Young Akin*, nor the modernized copy, *Young Hastings*, communicated by Buchan to Motherwell. Earlier and better renderings of the ballad have doubtless been lost. In the old Scottish speech, an Etin signified an ogre or giant, and although the existing versions show but faint traces of a supernatural element, it is probable that the original character of the story has been changed by the accidents of tradition, and that the Etin was at the outset in line with such personages as Arnold's Forsaken Merman. In the beautiful kindred ballads which abound in the Norse and German literatures, the Etin is sometimes represented by a merman, though usually by an elf-king, dwarf-king, or hill-king. *Hind chiel*, young stripling. *Spier*, ask. *Bigg*, build. *Their lane*, alone. *Brae*, hillside. *Gars*, makes. *Greet*, weep. *Stown*, stolen. *Laverock*, lark. *Lift*, air. *Buntin'*, blackbird. *Christendame*, christening. *Ben*, in. *Shaw*, forest. *Louted*, bowed. *Boun'*, go.

PAGE 177. **Lamkin.** After Jamieson. The many versions of this ballad show an unusually small number of variations. The name, though occurring in the several forms of Lambert Linkin, Lamerlinkin, Rankin, Belinkin, Lankyn, Lonkin, Balcanqual, most often appears as Lamkin or Lammikin or Lambkin, being perhaps a nick-name given to the mason for the meekness with which he had borne his injuries. This would explain the resentful tone of his inquiries on entering the house. *Nourice*, nurse. *Limmer*, wretch. *Shot-window*, projecting window. *Gaire*, edge of frock. *Ilka*, each. *Bore*, crevice. *Greeting*, crying. *Dowie*, doleful. *Chamer*, chamber. *Lamer*, amber. *Ava'*, of all.

P. 182. **Hugh of Lincoln.** Mainly after Jamieson. Percy gives a version of this famous ballad under title of *The Jew's Daughter*, and Herd and Motherwell, as well as Jamieson, have secured copies from recitation. The general view that this ballad rests upon an historical basis has but slender authority behind it. Matthew Paris, never too reliable as a chronicler, says that in 1255 the Jews of Lincoln, after their yearly custom, stole a little Christian boy, tortured and crucified him, and flung him into a pit, where his mother found the body. This is in all probability one of the many cruel slanders circulated against the Jews during the Middle Ages, to reconcile the Christian conscience to the Christian maltreatment of that long-suffering race. Such stories are related of various mediæval innocents, in various lands and centuries, and may be classed together, until better evidence to the contrary presents itself, as malicious falsehood. This ballad should be compared, of course, with Chaucer's *Prioresses Tale*. *Keppit*, caught. *Gart*, made. *Twinn'd*, deprived. *Row'd*, rolled. *Ilka*, each. *Gin*, if.

P. 185. **Fair Annie.** Mainly after Jamieson's version entitled *Lady Jane*. Jamieson gives another copy, where the heroic lady is known as *Burd Helen,* but Scott, Motherwell, Kinloch, Buchan, and others agree on the name *Fair Annie.* The pathetic beauty of the ballad has secured it a wide popularity. There are Danish, Swedish, Dutch, and German versions. "But Fair Annie's fortunes have not only been charmingly sung," says Professor Child. "They have also been exquisitely *told* in a favorite lay of Marie de France, 'Le Lai del Freisne.' This tale of Breton origin is three hundred years older than any manuscript of the ballad. Comparison will, however, quickly show that it is not the source either of the English or of the Low German and Scandinavian ballad. The tale and the ballads have a common source, which lies further back, and too far for us to find." *Your lane,* alone. *Braw,* finely dressed. *Gear,* goods. *But and,* and also. *Stown,* stolen. *Leugh,* laughed. *Loot,* let. *Gars,* makes. *Greet,* weep.

PAGE 189. **The Laird o' Drum.** After Aytoun's collated version. Copies obtained from recitation are given by Kinloch and Buchan. The eccentric Laird o' Drum was an actual personage, who, in the seventeenth century, mortified his aristocratic relatives and delighted the commons by marrying a certain Margaret Coutts, a woman of lowly rank, his first wife having been a daughter of the Marquis of Huntly. The old shepherd speaks in the Aberdeen dialect. *Weel-faur'd,* well-favored. *Gin,* if. *Speer,* ask. *Kebbuck,* cheese. *Yetts,* gates. *Gawsy,* portly. *But the pearlin' abune her bree,* without the lace above her brow.

P. 192. **Lizie Lindsey.** After Jamieson. Complete copies are given by Buchan and Whitelaw, also. *Till,* to. *Braes,* hills. *Fit,* foot. *Gin,* if. *Tocher,* dowry. *Gait,* way. *Wale,* choice. *Dey,* dairy-woman. *Laverock,* lark. *Liltin',* carolling. *Shealin',* sheepshed. *Gaits and kye,* goats and cows.

P. 196. **Katharine Janfarie.** Mainly after Motherwell's version entitled *Catherine Johnstone.* Other renderings are given by Scott, Maidment, and Buchan. In Scott's version the name of the English suitor is Lord Lochinvar, and both name and story the thieving poet has turned, as everybody knows, to excellent account. The two closing stanzas here seem to betray the hand of an English balladist. *Weel-faur'd,* well-favored. *Lave,* rest. *Spier'd,* asked. *Brae,* hill.

P. 199. **Glenlogie.** After Smith's version in the *Scottish Minstrel,* — a book wherein " great liberties," Motherwell claims, have been taken with ancient lays. A rough but spirited version is given by Sharpe, and a third by Buchan. *Gar,* make. *His lane,* alone.

PAGE 201. **Get up and Bar the Door.** After Herd. This ballad appears, too, in Johnson's *Museum* and Ritson's *Scottish Songs.* *Martinmas,* the eleventh of November. *Intil,* into. *Hussyskep,* house-keeping. *Bree,* broth. *Scaud,* scald.

P. 203. **The Lawlands o' Holland.** After Herd. Another version, longer and poorer, occurs in Johnson's *Museum. Withershins,* the wrong way. *Twinned,* parted.

P. 204. **The Twa Corbies.** After Scott, who received it from Mr. C. K. Sharpe, " as written down, from tradition, by a lady." This seems to be the Scottish equivalent of an old English poem, *The Three Ravens,* given by Ritson in his *Ancient Songs. Corbies,* ravens. *Fail,* turf. *Kens,* knows. *Hause,* neck. *Pyke,* pick. *Theek,* thatch.

P. 205. **Helen of Kirconnell.** After Scott. Other versions are given by Herd, Ritson, and Jamieson. There is said to be a traditional basis for the ballad, and the grave of the lovers, Adam Fleming and Helen Irving (or Helen Bell), is still pointed out in the churchyard of Kirconnell, near Springkell. *Burd,* lady.

P. 207. **Waly Waly.** After Ramsay, being first published in the *Tea-Table Miscellany.* These touching and tender stanzas have been pieced by Chambers into the patchwork ballad, *Lord Jamie Douglas,* but evidently it is not there that they belong. *Waly,* a cry of lamentation. *Brae,* hillside. *Burn,* brook. *Syne,* then. *Lichtly,* slight. *Busk,* adorn. *Marti'mas,* November. *Fell,* bitterly. *Cramasie,* crimson.

P. 208. **Lord Ronald.** After Scott's version entitled *Lord Randal.* Scott adopts this name because he thinks the ballad may originally have had reference to the death of Thomas Randolph, or Randal, Earl of Murray, — a theory which Allingham, with more justice than mercy, briefly disposes of as " mere antiquarian moonshine." In point of fact the ballad recounts an old, old story, told in many literatures, Italian, German, Dutch, Swedish, Danish, Magyar, Wendish, Bohemian, Catalan. The English offshoot takes on a bewildering variety of forms. (See Introduction, pp. xiii, xiv.) *Broo',* broth.

P. 209. **Edward, Edward.** After Percy, the ballad having made its first appearance in the *Reliques.* Motherwell gives an interesting version, in which the murderer, who in this case has slain his brother, is addressed as *Son Davie.* There are German, Swedish, Danish and Finish equivalents. The old orthography, which is retained here for its literary interest, cannot obscure the tragic power of the ballad. *Frie,* free. *Dule ye drie,* grief ye suffer. *Tul,* till.